*Scottish
Festivals*

Scottish Festivals

Sheila Livingstone

Birlinn

First published in Great Britain, 1997 by
Birlinn Limited
14 High Street
Edinburgh EH1 1TE

ISBN 1 874744 78 5

British Library Cataloguing-in-Publication Data
A Catalogue record of this book is available
from the British Library

Designed and typeset in 10/12pt Horley Old Style
by Janet Watson

Made and printed in Finland by
Werner Söderström OY

Contents

Introduction

Scotland celebrates, in common with most countries, certain festivals. Nowadays the meaning behind the majority of them has been obscured and they have deteriorated into an excuse for a holiday or a day for children to have some fun and enjoyment. For centuries these festivals, many of which were based on seasonal events and followed the course of the sun, were very serious occasions on which the people based their hopes for prosperity and good crops in the following year.

Many festivals, such as Beltane and Hallowe'en, or Samhain were Celtic in origin. These were fire festivals to mark the power of the sun to enrich and renew the crops and to mourn its disappearance leaving the earth dead. Yule which covers the period of Christmas and New Year continued until the old New Year, January the sixth – Twelfth Night, which was of Scandinavian origin. The Scots have absorbed folklore from both cultures. In the west the Celtic is strongest while in the north-east and Orkney and Shetland, the Norse or Scandinavian is uppermost.

Roman culture also had an influence on Scottish celebrations. *Feriae* meant holiday in Latin and applied to festivals held on the feast days of Saints. During the sixth century A.D. Pope Gregory sent St Augustine to Britain as a missionary with the instruction to adapt the old customs to Christianity.

*The heathen temples were not to be destroyed, but turned into
Christian churches; that the oxen killed in sacrifice should be
killed with rejoicing, but their bodies given to the poor, and that
the refreshment booths round the heathen temples should be
allowed to remain as places of jollity and amusement for the
people on Christian festivals, for it is impossible to cut abruptly
from hard and rough minds all their old habits and customs.*

Folklore or Superstitious Beliefs in the West of Scotland within this Century,
James Napier, 1879

These feasts, which were held up until the Reformation, in the
sixteenth century, as well as being religious occasions usually
had other celebrations attached to them. Once the religious
side of things had been attended to the people took the chance
to enjoy themselves as, on these occasions, they were usually
granted a holiday from work.Gradually the celebration of the
saint fell away but the day remained and was held as a fair which
eventually also lost its main purpose as a place to buy and sell
goods and animals and became a showground or carnival. This
was the reason that fairs were originally held within the
churchyard although later they expanded into the streets and
eventually to a nearby field or park.

*Enjoyments they had – at their Fastern's E'en, their
Hallowmas, their fairs, and their Sacraments – those
Holy Fairs associated with scarcely less excitement.*

The Social Life of Scotland in the Eighteenth Century, H.G. Graham,1899

Despite the efforts of the Church to force the people to abandon
their saints days these festivals were so deeply entrenched that
the habits continued. On Saints' days after the Reformation
many old customs were still practised.

*Twenty years after the Reformation, [1581] days of idolatry,
pilgrimages to wells, observing festival days of the sancts,
sometimes namit their patrons; setting forth banefires [and]
singing carols within and about kirks at ane certaine time of
the year.*

Domestic Annals of Scotland, Vol 1, From the Revolution to the Rebellion 1745,
Robert Chambers, 1874

An Act of Parliament was passed in 1581 against the lighting of bonfires on such days but this did not eliminate the practice.

However in 1618 King James VI declared that Sunday sports should be permitted and dancing, either by men or women, archery for men, leaping and vaulting should take place. May Games, Maypoles, Whitsun-ales and Morris dancing should be allowed so long as those who participated had attended church in the morning because:

This prohibition barreth the common meaner people from using such exercises as may make their bodies more able for war, when we or our successors shall have occasion to use them, and, in place therof, sets up filthy tipplings and drunkeness, and breeds a number of idle and dicontented speeches in their ale-houses; for when shall the common people have leave to exercise, if not upon the Sundays and holidays, seeing they must apply their labour, and win their living on other days.
Domestic Annals of Scotland, Vol 1, From the Revolution to the Rebellion 1745,
Robert Chambers, 1874

Other festivals developed from legal formalities such as the inspection of the boundaries of a town or village or the need for training young men in the defence of their clan or country. These survive as ceremonies such as the Riding of the Marches, in Highland Gatherings and in parades and processions, which were originally observed by trades and craftsmen.

There are many customs attached to these occasions, some are now carried out in a watered down form more by habit than with any sense of their meaning while others do still have a symbolic meaning which is quite clear. Many festivals and fairs have disappeared while more and more are being revived as people investigate the past of their own locality.

Spring and summer festivals involved seeds, greenery and flowers while those held in autumn were a celebration of a good harvest and plenty grain in store. Winter festivals involved lights as a reminder that the sun would return. Many customs which nowadays have become attached to a particular festival were carried out on most celebratory occasions. First-footing, divination, guising, hidden trinkets, dancing around fires, bringing greenery indoors for luck were part of every quarter day as well as being carried out on specific occasions such as Beltane, Hallowe'en and Yule.

The Scots adopted the Norwegian custom of beginning a festival day at sunset on the previous night, and ending it at sunset on the following day.

In Scotland we have to give thanks to the many writers who recorded and investigated the habits and customs of their time and locality, to Kirk Session Records which are available for many parishes and especially to those ministers of the Church of Scotland who in the eighteenth and nineteenth centuries wrote systematically about their parish. These accounts were gathered into a priceless asset, *The First Statistical Account of Scotland*, in 1796 and *The Second Statistical Account of Scotland*, 1854.

This book covers festivals and other public occasions while *Scottish Customs*, a companion volume, goes into more detail about divination rights, and beliefs about luck, superstitious actions and the healing powers of plants, water and stones.

Sheila Livingstone, 1996

Spring

*F*estivals were important occasions and possible 'cracks in time' so everyone was on their guard against fairies and witches. To protect the house a twig of rowan was placed over the lintel of the door and over the byre. Nothing was ever lent on a quarter day in case the luck of the house went with it. Some customs were carried out both at Candlemas Day and Fastern's Eve as well as, in the Highlands and Islands in particular, on St Bride's Day. Games such as football and handball were played, divination took place, cock-fights were held and dancing and fun were the order of the day.

ST BRIDE'S DAY

Day of Bride

February the first was dedicated to St Bride, the Christian form of the earlier Bridget or Briganta who was the Celtic goddess of the hearth, healing, marriage, childbirth and poetry. This was a festival to celebrate the return of spring when the goddess was rescued by the ever youthful Angus from her captivity in Ben Nevis where she was taken by the 'Cailleach' or Blue Hag of winter on Hallowe'en. Bride and Angus had the same father, the Dagda, god of fertility and agriculture.

The Eve of Bride

The women and girls of the community dressed a sheaf of corn as a woman. Twelve maidens dressed in white carried their Bride from door to door. Everyone added a gift, a shiny shell, a crystal, primroses, snowdrops. Mothers prepared a Bride Bannock and cheese which the girls placed in one house to which they returned. Here they chose the brightest crystal as the Star of Bride which they placed on her breast. They then had a feast. Bride was displayed in the window as a signal to the young men who came to the house begging admittance. They had to bow to her, then dancing and games followed. In the morning the remainder of the gifts were distributed to the poorer women of the community.

The older women made a bed for Bride, a cradle was dressed and the Bride put into it. A wand of birch, a sacred wood, was placed in her hand.

> *Anna sat with the side of her face to him, knitting, and while she made the needles flash she rocked a wicker cradle with her foot and sang.*
>
> > *O Bride, Brideag, come with the wand*
> > *To this wintry land;*
> > *And breathe with the breath of the Spring so bland,*
> > *Bride, Bride, little Bride! . . .*
>
> *'I declare Miss Anna,' said Duncan, 'that I could not find you better engaged. The baby and you must pardon me for spoiling the song.' 'The Baby!' cried Anna, and seeing he was in earnest laughed outright. 'Bonny on the baby! Come and see our Brideag!' She tilted over the wicker cradle and let him see it held only a sheaf of corn, ornamented with flowers and shells and ribbons. 'Have you been so long in France,' she asked, still laughing. . . 'that you have forgotten the little Bride?'*
>
> Children of Tempest, Neil Munro, 1905

Bride was always formally invited into the house to give her blessing.

Omens

The morning after the Day of Bride the women scanned the ashes looking for omens. It was lucky if there was a mark or footprint as it meant that Bride had blessed the house and luck would follow. The oyster catcher and the lintie were thought to be Bride's birds because they whistled and sang on that day.

CANDLEMAS

Candlemas was originally a festival for the return of spring held by the Romans in honour of Februa, the daughter of Mars. They carried torches through the city on February the first. The Greeks also held torchlight processions to honour Ceres, mother of Proserpine, who was believed to have searched for her daughter, taken into the Underworld on that day. This festival was christianized as the Purification of the Virgin Mary and was held on February the second.

Candlemas Pageants

Crafts associations and guilds held processions in the Middle Ages in honour of Our Lady and at St Andrew's University, the Kate Kennedy Procession, now held in April, was originally held on Candlemas Day.

Candlemas bleeze

In many areas school pupils barred the gates against the master to keep him out until he granted them a half-holiday. It was traditional for pupils to give a gift to the schoolmaster on this day. Originally this was a peat used to provide heating, therefore a blaze or 'bleeze' which through time developed into a bonfire, or they brought a large candle which could give a good light. Somewhere along the line it changed into cash and a cockerel.

> *Douce Elder John, than ca's the names,*
> *The bairnies than do ease;*
> *Their pouches wagging by their wames,*
> *Wi' their intended bleeze;*
> *Some saxpence brass – a shilling bit,*
> *An' some gie twa or three;*
> *Gif that they be inclined to sit,*
> *As king and queen ye see,*
> *Upon this day.*
>
> *Scottish Gallovidian Encyclopedia*, John Mactaggart, 1824

At Southwick in Galloway, the Bleeze was an actual bonfire where an effigy of Tom Paine the Infidel, the political reformer, was burnt.

Offerings

In city and burgh schools there was a humiliating custom whereby the schoolmaster sat at his desk to receive the monetary offerings. If sixpence to two shillings Scots was laid down it was greeted in silence. When two and sixpence appeared, equal to a quarter's fee, the master shouted *'Vivat!'*; five shillings – *'Floreat bis!'*; a higher amount was greeted with *'Floreat ter!'* If a wealthy boy gave ten shillings the cry was *'Gloriat!'* In 1785, Glasgow Town Council ruled that this custom of differentiating between the offerings must stop.

Candlemas crown

This was a badge of distinction, sometimes an actual tin crown, given to the pupil at a grammar school who gave the highest amount to the rector.

> *The scholars pay . . . a Candlemas gratuity, according to their rank and fortune, from 5/- even as far as five guineas where there is keen competition for the Candlemas crown.*
> Parish of Fife, First Statistical Account of Scotland, 1795

Candlemas king and queen

The honour of being crowned Candlemas king and queen went to the boy and girl who offered the most money to the school-master. The Candlemas king reigned for six weeks, during which time he could demand an afternoon of play once-a-week and if he so wished he could cancel any punishments.

Food and drink

Parents were invited to attend the school as also were the kirk elders where they were served cheese, oatcakes and whisky or punch.

> *Roun comes the jug on whiteairn trays,*
> *The sweet brewn whusky toddy;*
> *'Come whomeld owre,' the waiter says,*
> *'T'will hurt na' honest body;'*

> *Than Carvie Kebbuck featly cut*
> *In sonsy oblong dasses,*
> *Wi' bruckelie sely owre the glut,*
> *What stiveron this surpasses,*
> *Nane-nane, nae day.*
>
> Scottish Gallovidian Encyclopedia, John Mactaggart, 1824

The schoolmaster often gave his pupils a gift of oranges and a bun on Candlemas Eve.

Cockfighting

This custom also took place on Fastern's E'en in some areas. The town council of Dumfries, in 1725, issued rules:

> *The under teacher keep the door and exact not more than twelve pennies Scots from each scholar for the benefit of bringing a cockerel to fight in the schoolroom; and that none be suffered to enter that day except gentlemen and persons of note from whom nothing is to be demanded; and what money is given by the scholars, the under teacher is to receive and apply to his own use for his pains and trouble; and that no scholar except who pleases shall furnish a cockerel; but that all scholars whether they have a cockerel or not can enter the school. Those having none paying 2/- Scots as a forfeit.*
>
> History of Dumfries, J. McDowall, 18 67

The schoolmaster was allowed to keep the birds which were killed or wounded in the cockfight. For weeks the boys trained their cockerels so that they would be fit for the fight.

> *Given to John Erskine to buy a cock to fight on Fastern's*
> *E'en – 6/-*
>
> Household Book, Dowager Countess of Mar, 1638

Although outlawed, this was a popular pastime in Scotland for centuries.

> *Nae matter tho' they now a ring,*
> *Do form fu' wide and braw,*
> *And into it their cock's they fling,*
> *The chanticleers do craw;*
> *But aiblins there is ane o'm game,*

Steel spur'd in fighting order;
Sae some saft faes he soon does tame,
And some my chap does murder,
Perchance that day.

Scottish Gallovidian Encyclopedia, John Mactaggart, 1824

In Glasgow the aristocracy patronised this sport. In 1783 there was a well-known cockpit at Rutherglen Bridge which was a favourite with the Duke of Hamilton and a building for cockfighting was erected in Hope Street, Glasgow in 1835. It housed 280 people plus judges, handlers and feeders. 'Senators to journeymen butchers' were said to attend and a great deal of money changed hands in bets. In 1661 *Mercurious Caledonius* records:

> *Our carnival sports are in some measure revived, for according to ancient custom the work was carried on by cockfighting in the schools, and in the streets among the vulgar sort, tilting at cockerels with fagot-sticks.*

Domestic Annals of Scotland, Vol 2, From the Revolution to the Rebellion 1745,
Robert Chambers, 1874

Cock-throwing

This was another cruel practice, when these 'fugies', cockerels which refused to fight, were tied to a stake in the school yard and pelted with stones until they were killed. The boys had to pay a half-penny Scots for each shot, the money was collected and given to the schoolmaster along with the carcasses. His family lived on roasted cockerel for weeks.

Burnt Candlemas

This was the name given to the act of revenge taken on Candlemas Eve against William, Lord of Douglas, by King Edward III, in 1356, when he burned down every abbey, church and town from the Borders up to Haddington.

Candlemas Ba'

This was another popular sport played either as football or handball, from Banff to Kirkcudbright. At Kelso the 'King' was presented with a football by the teachers and rector of the school. It was often dressed with ribbons which were eventually torn into pieces and the young men wore these in their hat brims or lapels.

Mock valentines

These were cards, exchanged during Candlemas in Campbeltown, which were often rude and were disliked by many people.

FASTERN'S E'EN

This was the only true 'carnival' – the farewell to meat. It was held on the last Tuesday before Lent, which was known in England as Shrove Tuesday. This feast was a way of using up fat and butter as well as meat which was made into beef brose. In Scotland the day had several names such as Beef Brose and Bannock Night, Brosie, Sautie Bannock Night, Rappy Night, Shriften E 'en and Fastern E'en.

> First come Candlemas, then the new meen,
> The next Tuesday efter is aye Fastern's Een.

Traditional

It was an excuse for fun before the sacrifices of Lent. People gathered together, in farmtoun, in houses, in town and country, to have a good time. In some towns there were processions of craftsmen, in others games of football or handball were played in the streets. At night there would be music and dancing and, of course, eating and drinking.

Football or handball

Teams of men from opposite ends of the town or village – unmarried men versus married men or one trade against another – took part in games of football, a tradition dating back to the Middle Ages when the clergy also took part.

> Item on Fasternis-Evin, to ane fule with the treyn [wooden sword], -18d, to the pyper callet Ryall Dayis for playing, -18d, item to John Andro for sax futeballis, 12/-

Glasgow Treasurer's Account, 1576

In the middle of the eighteenth century a decision was taken to change to handball to save life and limb. In 1848 an attempt was made in Jedburgh to outlaw the Callant's Ba', held at Candlemas and the Men's Ba', held on Fastern's E'en, when the 'uppies' played the 'doonies', but this was overturned by the court.

Jedburgh handba' is a mass game and the ball is carried in tempestuous scrambles through houses and shops. The locked crowd of players sway through the streets past barricaded windows. It is a free-for-all and all-in and the players are legion. The major, if not the only rule, and it is apparently unwritten, is that injuries should not be inflicted deliberately.

It's an Old Scottish Custom, Neil McCallum, n.d.

Kirk or Mill

There was great rivalry on these occasions. At Duns, Berwickshire the ball was 'either kirked or milled' which meant that the players tried to place the ball either in the pulpit of the church or in the happer of the mill.

If the ball was deposited in the happer, the miller entertained the victors to pork and 'dumplins''' and dusted their hats with flour.

The Silver Bough, Vol. 2, F. M. McNeill, 1957/68

There were great dances held afterwards and people enjoyed themselves until the wee sma' hours.

At Duns the game was transferred to the Wednesday of Reivers' Week held in June.

Maintenance of the ball

At Strathearn a young couple on their wedding day had to give money towards the upkeep of the football. In many of the crafts associations, entry to the guild included money for this purpose.

Rocking

In rural areas on Fastern's Eve the girls and older women would gather together and gossip, while sitting knitting or spinning with their roks and distaffs, to be joined later by the menfolk when the party would begin.

At Fastern's Eve we had a rockin'
To ca' the crack and weave our stockin';
And there was muckle fun and jokin',
Ye needna doubt;
At length we had a hearty yokin'
At sang about.

Epistle to J. Lapraik, Robert Burns, 1785

Food and drink

The main food was beef. Brose, made the day before called Collop Day, was a thick soup made with vegetables and all the pieces of meat left in the larder. Sauty bannocks and pancakes were favourites.

He and McKail came in to get some salt cakes bak'd it being Fastern Even.

Session Records, Parish of Maybole, 1870

Mill-bannocks

A mill-bannock, which was a large thick oatcake about a foot in diameter, with a hole in the centre, was made by the miller. It was toasted on the burning seeds of shelled oats or on kelp which was said to give it a wonderful flavour. Dumplings made of oatmeal rolled into balls and boiled were also eaten. Whisky and ale were in demand and sometimes a spicy punch was made.

Beef Brose

Beef Brose and Bannock Day was a popular celebration. A large piece of meat was tied up and boiled over the fire. When cooked, it was placed next to the peat fire to roast. The fat was skimmed off and poured over oatmeal, already prepared in a separate dish, to which a ring had been added. This was called brose. The head of the house, his family and all his employees, plus any neighbours who had been invited, sat down to a dinner of brose, followed by meat and potatoes.

Fasterns E'en dinner

In Edinburgh, in 1661, it was recorded by *Mercurious Caledonius*, one of the earliest journals, that the gentry would invite guests in the evening and enjoy a feast.

Lusty caudles, powerful cock-broth and natural crammed pullets, a divertisement not much inferior to our neighbour nation's fritters and pancakes.

Domestic Annals of Scotland, Vol 2, From the Revolution to the Rebellion 1745, Robert Chambers, 1874

Grace

A traditional grace would be said:

> *Grace be here, and grace be there,*
> *And grace be on the table,*
> *Ilka one tak' up their speen*
> *An' sup a' that they're able*
> Traditional

or

> *Some hae meat an' canny eat*
> *An some wad eat that want it,*
> *But we hae meat, an' we can eat,*
> *An' sae the Lord be thankit.*
> Traditional

Divination

Brose

The young enjoyed several ways of finding out who would be their future partners. The ring which was put into the brose, in some areas, was searched for by the young men and women who, carrying their own horn spoons, visited round the houses and supped the soup hoping to find the ring. The first to find it would be married that year but it was unlucky to announce that the find had been made.

Dreaming bannock

A dreaming bannnock meant that extra salt had to be added to the mixture and it was filled with trinkets before being fired. In some places soot was added for luck. The salt was supposed to ensure dreaming of a loved one. The bannock was broken into pieces and carried round the unmarried who had to choose a piece. The trinkets were a thimble, ring, button or coin, and each foretold a different fate – an old maid, a marriage, a bachelor or wealth. If nothing at all was found it would not be a good year.

> *I ground it in a quern on Friday*
> *I baked it on a fan of sheepskin*
> *I toasted it on a fire of rowan*
> *And I shared it round my people.*
> Traditional

10

Pieces of the bannock were taken home and placed in the toe of the left sock or stocking and put under the pillow to dream on in the hope that a future spouse would appear.

Dumb cake

The dumb cake was an individual pancake which was made by each unmarried person dropping a spoonful of the mixture onto the hot girdle, turning it and lifting it off without saying a word. It was always made with the eggs left over after having been used for divination. The others had to try to make them speak by asking them questions. Other forms of divination, now associated mainly with Hallowe'en, were also carried out.

Rappy night

Youngsters always enjoy an excuse to play tricks on their elders. In Aberdeenshire as late as 1908 they locked the teachers out and sang

> *Beef brose and bannock day*
> *Please give us a half-holiday.*
> Traditional

Door tapping

The young ones would go into the fields and pull white ball turnips, including their shaws. After dark they would sneak out and knock on a neighbour's door with the turnip head and run away yelling when the occupant came to investigate.

Window tapping

Another favourite was window tapping. In Forfar they called it 'the skeleton's rapping at the windie'. This was usually carried out with a long piece of thread which was attached to the window with wax or , in modern times, chewing gum. A small stone or button was threaded through and fixed about a foot from the top. The rest of the thread hung loose. When the thread was pulled the object tapped the window and hopefully brought the occupant to the door. The idea was not to be seen or caught.

Chicky Mellie

A selection rhyme was used. All the boys taking part held out their clenched fists. One boy would chant a rhyme and touch one fist for each word. At the end of it the last fist to be hit had to be put behind the owner's back. When two fists were 'out' that person was excluded. The process continued until only one person was left. This one had to carry out the deed.

Rhymes used were:

> *Eenty, teentie*
> *figgery fell*
> *Ell, dell, dominell*
> *Urky purky, taury rope*
> *An tan, tausy Jock*
> *You are out.*
>
> Traditional

or

> *Eatum, peetum, penny pie*
> *Cock-a-lorie, jinty jye*
> *Staan ye oot by*
> *For a bonnie penny pie*
>
> Traditional

The prank called chicky mellie consisted of finding a milk bottle and filling it with water and sand or gravel. It was then placed above a door. A piece of string was attached to it and was also tied to the door knob. The door was knocked and on answering it the bottle smashed making a terrible mess and frightening the householder.

Door tying

In Angus a rope was tied to two neighbouring door handles. The doorbells were rung in the hope that both occupants would open them at the same time and feel a tug as though someone was pulling it from outside. The really brave then cut the rope and ran away.

Sowening

In Aberdeenshire doors and windows might be plastered with a substance made from sowens, which was made from the coarser particles of oatmeal returned to the farmer by the miller along with his meal. It was put on with a whitewash brush.

These tricks were practised on a variety of occasions when dressing up and going guising was permitted. Usually they were carried out on the least popular people in the town or village, those who would were mean or grumpy.

St Valentine's Day

On February the fourteenth children went around the houses and begged for sweets, money or fruit. Their older brothers and sisters were more interested in finding a sweetheart. In some places name-papers were used to speed up the process. These were bits of paper on which the name of a boy or a girl was written. They were placed in a bonnet and each person drew one, read it and returned it to the bonnet. If the same name was drawn out three times it meant that a marriage would take place. Another use of the name-paper was to take it to the house of the chosen girl and hand it in. On delivery an apple was traditionally given in exchange. Gloves were sometimes given as a present on St Valentine's Day.

Whuppity Scoorie

This was held in Lanark on March the first and was a survival of the belief that making a great din frightened away the fairies and evil spirits. It may also represent the battle of spring over winter. The church bells did not ring at six o'clock from October until the last day of February. On March the first the custom was resumed. Money was given each year by the town council from the Common Good Fund for pennies which were scrambled. The children waited eagerly for the coins to be thrown and pushed and shoved to retrieve them from the ground.

Balls made of rolled-up paper tied with string were swung around their heads as they ran around the church three times deasil, hitting one another with their missiles, until the bells stopped. At one time the young men took part but latterly it became a festival for children. The youths did not use balls but bonnets attached to a string. They fought with the lads from New Lanark.

The children were too impatient to wait for the bell to be rung, and started running as soon as the clock had struck six. It was impossible to stop them in this wild flight, but when they had

completed their unauthorized rounds, they were made to
repeat the three-fold run before the pennies were thrown
for the scramble.

Hamilton Advertiser, 6 March 1964

EASTER OR PASCH

Pasch, pace or pess was the old Scots name for the festival
now called Easter which is derived from the Jewish Pesach –
Passover. Pasch was a celebration of the return of spring and
the rebirth of the natural world.

> *First comed Candlemas, an' then the new meen,*
> *The first Tuesday efter that is aye Fastern's Een,*
> *That meen oot an' the neist meen's hicht,*
> *An' the first Sunday efter that is aye Pess richt.*

Traditional

In England this was originally a festival to honour Eastre, a
Saxon goddess of fertility. It became Christian in the fourth
century A.D. and celebrated as Easter; a moveable festival, its
date related to Lent and fell between March the twenty-first
and April the twenty-fifth. It was rarely called Easter in
Scotland until the nineteenth century.

Good Friday

> *Pasch Day, or Easter day should be included within Lentron*
> *time, because it was now holden superstitious; nor nae*
> *communion given on Good Friday nor this Pasch Day, as*
> *was usit before. Marvellous in Aberdeen to see no market,*
> *fowl or flesh to be sold on Pasch Even.*

Domestic Annals of Scotland, Vol 2, From the Revolution to the Rebellion 1745,
Robert Chambers, 1874

On this day ploughing was avoided, blacksmiths did not work
on Good Friday and no seed was sown. It was also considered
unlucky to go to sea on Good Friday.

14

Food and drink
Hot cross buns
These were originally baked for the old festival and, when the people, especially in the Highlands, would not give up this custom, the Christian Church adapted it by having them make the mark of the cross on them. The buns are highly spiced and often contain dried fruit. Nowadays the cross is usually made of pastry.

Pancakes
Pancakes made of eggs, milk, meal or flour were baked for Easter Sunday. Eggs and butter were forbidden during Lent after which they were welcomed once more into their diet:

'On Pess-day I'll get twa big hard-boiled eggs instead o' saps.'

Bread of mane
This was a loaf baked with fine flour on which a figure of Jesus or the Virgin Mary was impressed.

Pace eggs
At one time eggs were collected by the poor who had no poultry of their own. They went around the farms asking for their pace eggs. Later this was adopted by children who visited relatives and friends hoping to be given a coloured egg which they knew would be prepared for them.

Treasure hunts
In some places finding the eggs was made into a game and adults would hide them about the farm, wood or garden for the children to hunt.

Dyeing
Children looked forward to their eggs which were hard-boiled and dyed by using natural materials such as bracken, heather and a variety of other plants. Whin gave yellow, onions – brown. Tea-leaves were also used. Wax from a candle was sometimes put on before dyeing to make a pattern.

Exchanging eggs
Eggs of different colours could be exchanged. Girls placed them on their aprons and, on meeting their friends, proceeded to trade eggs.

Pesse pie
This was a chicken pie decorated with chicken feathers which was eaten at Eastertime.

Wooden eggs
These began to appear in the late nineteenth century and were usually of two sections which when opened contained a small trinket.

Chocolate eggs
These, often elaborately designed eggs, are now popular and are given as gifts at Easter time.

Biscuits
Children also enjoyed the excitement of waiting beside a boat or ship which was going to sea after Easter. Sailors always took something which was baked on Good Friday to sea with them. Sometimes this was a form of dry biscuit and they would throw a piece ashore for luck.

Pace clothes
It was traditional to wear a new piece of clothing at Easter, especially a new bonnet. In some areas it was believed that unless a person wore one new item at Easter they would die before the next one came round. Those who could not afford anything new were called pace-yauds.

The King's outfit
In 1495, King James VI's Easter outfit was a doublet of two colours made in crimson and black satin. He wore a jacket of crimson velvet, and had scarlet stockings. His black velvet gown (cloak) was trimmed with crimson velvet. His attendants had gowns of green with black stockings while the yeomen wore blue gowns with doublets of white fustian and black stockings. The trumpeters wore green also. One year the colours chosen for Easter were black and rowan red, a sort of orange.

Pasch Sunday

In June 1625, the Presbytery of Lanark exercised discipline upon John Baillie, William Baillie, John Hirshaw, John and

*Thomas Prentices, and Robert Watt, a piper, profaners of the
Sabbath in fetching hame a Maypole, and dancing about the
same on Pasch Sunday.*

Registers of the Presbytery of Lanark, 1618

Easter Monday

Although originally eggs were rolled on Easter Sunday this
was often carried out on Easter Monday when picnics were
taken to a 'paiss-brae', any sloping piece of ground where eggs
were rolled down. The last one to break was the winner. If they
were not damaged too badly the eggs were then eaten. This in its
later Christian form represented the rolling away of the stone
from the tomb of Jesus.

Divination

In the Hebrides the eggs were marked to identify their owners.
They were then rolled. The egg which ran the furthest was the
luckiest. All eggs unbroken were lucky but if the egg was
smashed it meant bad luck before the year's end. At Connel
Ferry the lads and girls chose separate hills. The egg which ran
the furthest indicated that the owner would be the first to marry.

Maundy Thursday

On Maundy Thursdaythe herds cut a cleft in a piece of rowan
wood and attached a cross piece. They then laid them aside
until May Day when they decorated these sticks with herbs and
placed them on top of the byre door.

Gruel Day

On Maundy Thursday, the fishing communities of the Western
Isles made an offering of gruel and a honey drink, which they
made the previous year with the harvest from the bees, to
Shony, the sea god. This was to ensure that there would be
another fruitful year. They depended on the seaweed for
fertiliser to help their crops to grow.

Skyre Thursday

This was held before the Reformation on March the twenty-
eighth. 'Keir' meant holy and there was a Scare [sic] Thursday
Fair held at Melrose amongst other places. It was recorded on

Skyre Thursday, in 1581, twenty years after the Reformation, that a Monsieur de Menainville, from Picardy, called thirteen poor men into his lodgings in Edinburgh and washed their feet according to the Popish manner. This gave great offence to many people.

Taillie Day

On Deeside this was held on March the thirtieth and in Kirkcaldy on April the second . Tricks were played on people by fixing paper tails to the back of their clothes. The wearer went about unaware until someone called out 'Taillie! Taillie!'. If a boy managed to put the tail on the teacher or the minister, his status grew with his peers.

Huntigowk

The first of April is known as Huntigowk. It is a day when, up until noon, people try to catch each other out by telling them lies and by playing tricks which make them look foolish. The name is believed to come from an old trick where a person is sent out with a message:

> Dinna laugh, an' dinna smile
> But hunt the gowk another mile.
> Traditional

The 'gowk' is another name for the cuckoo, which is given the image of being a silly bird. At each stop the message bearer is sent on to someone else.

Tricks

The switchboards at the Scottish zoos are inundated with phone-calls asking to speak to Mr Lion or Mr Swan. Apprentices are sent in search of a left-handed screwdriver or tartan paint and people are told that their buttons are undone, their shoe-lace is untied or they discover that they have been wearing a notice on their back saying, 'Please kick me?'

Newspapers

Newspapers often join in the fun by printing articles about amazing finds or strange animals being sighted or some other almost believable nonsense.

Summer

Beltane

The name Baal was the appellation given by the Phoenicians, to their gods; hence, Baal-Zebub – lord of the flies, Baal-Shamish – lord of disguise; it was also the name of a fertility god of the Semites. In Babylonia he was called Bel and in Celtic belief Belenos. Fire was the earthly symbol associated with these gods so it was thought by many academics that this was the origin of Beltane. Others dispute this and believe that it was solely connected with the sun worship of the Druids, a bright fire in honour of the return of the sun. It was a festival for fertility to encourage the crops to grow and the cattle to thrive.

Sun and fire were sacred to the Druids who worshipped the sun by sacrificing animals and humans to this god. They believed in the power of fire to cleanse and to give protection from evil. Fire had the power to keep wild animals, witches and fairies away from their flocks so they drove the herd through the flames, an action which they believed surrounded them with this power. It also protected them from disease.

Beltane was also the festival of the return of summer, a time when the cattle were taken up to the higher pastures to feed on the new grass. Herds lived in the shielings from Beltane until Hallowe'en. Both these festivals were looked forward to and many of the rituals which were once of great significance eventually were retained just for fun.

The Romans also held a flower festival, Floralia, on the first of May, the rites of which came to be celebrated in the southeast of Scotland. This was a gentler festival, more like the English May Day but the rites of both festivals became mixed over the years.

Date of Beltane

May the first is usually given as the date on which Beltane was held but in some documents it is given as May the second, May the third or even as June the twenty-first which was the date on which it was held in Ireland. In many areas May the eighth was also called the Beltane.

The Roman Catholic Church tried to translate this feast into Rood Day, May the third to encourage the people to celebrate the Invention of the Cross. This was also the name given in some areas to the midsummer festival, which may account for the discrepancies.

> *On the first of May every village holds its Beltane*
> Tour in Scotland, T. Pennant, 1769

> *Three fairs . . . the first thereof beginning yearly upon the third day of May, called Beltane.*
> Royal Charter, Granted to the Burgh of Peebles, 1621

John Mactaggart in his *Scottish Gallovidian Encyclopedia* mentions Belton, May the third. It was a day on which bogles and fairies were given a free hand and the need to be vigilant was important. A second Beltane is also mentioned which was held on the May the eighth and several remarks are to be found of happenings 'between the Beltanes'.

Rood Day

A day dedicated to the Holy Cross was instituted by Constantine and celebrated on May the third. Churches, especially in cities, were named Holyrood. In areas where the Roman Catholic faith was powerful, such as in the cities or royal burghs, Rood Day became an important festival. There was also a Rood Day in Lent:

This is the day they ca' the Rood-Mass and the morn the
Beltane, and it behoves decent bodies to be indoors at the
darkenin' on Beltane's Eve. My faither was a bauld man, but
he widna have stirred a fit over his ain doorstep on the night o'
Rood-Mass for a king's ransom. There's anither Beltane on the
aucht day of May, and till that's by we maun walk eidently.
Witchwood, John Buchan, 1924

In some places it was known as Red E'en or the eve of Rood Day.
The Rood Day in barlan, was held at the time of the sewing of
the oats in Caithness. Rood Day in hairst (harvest), September
the fourteenth, celebrated the exultation of the Cross.

Bogles, whilk a' body kens are gi'en a free dispensation on Rood
Mass E'en.
Witchwood, John Buchan, 1924

Place names
The custom of lighting fires at certain places is reflected in
place names such as Tarbolton in Ayrshire (Tor = hill, Bolton =
Beltane), Tullybelton in Perthshire (*Tillie* = knoll, *betteine* =
Beltane), Ardentinny in Argyll (*Ard* = light, *an teine* = fire) and
Tinto in Lanarkshire (*Teinteach* = place of the fire).

Beltane fires
On the hills throughout Scotland at the beginning of May fires
were lit in celebration of the return of summer.

On [the] eve of May Day it was customary to light large fires
and burn furze bushes and heather. It was called Red-Even in
this Parish, but in many places it is known as Beltein-Eve.
History of Cairnie Parish, M.J. Pirie, 1897

Two fires of sacred woods such as rowan, oak or birch were built
and lit on the highest local hill. A passageway was left between
them and it was through this that the cattle were driven. This
was thought to be a watered down version of the Druidic
custom of sacrificing animals to the gods.

Need fire
The fires of Beltane had to be lit without the assistance of a flint
so two sticks were ground together until by natural friction a

spark appeared. This was used to kindle the fire at sunrise. Everyone put out their domestic fires before departing for the hill, driving their stock in front of them. They lit torches from the Beltane fire and after dancing three times deasil, or sunwise, around it they carried this torch or an ember from the fire into their own homes to kindle a new fire which hopefully would never be extinguished during the year. If the brand went out on the way home or if the domestic fire did not light this was considered unlucky and death or disaster would follow.

Tarbolton
On the night preceeding the Tarbolton Fair, which was later held in June, the young lads went around the doors asking for a piece of fuel which they took to build an altar; this was about three feet in height, set on a circle of turf on a nearby hill where the Celtic god, Bel, had been worshipped long ago. The old and young congregated to watch the young men leap over the bonfire when it was lit.

Beltane Fire Festival
The celebration of Beltane was revived in 1988 on Calton Hill, Edinburgh by modern-day New Age pagans, the Beltane Fire collective. This event attracts a number of groups including one mainly of women called the White Warrior Group. They pass through arches of fire, meet the Red Man and kill, symbolically, the Green Man of myth. There is a May Queen, only a sacred wood is used and greenery and all the trappings of the traditional centuries-old festival. Attendance of performers and spectators grows every year.

Sacrifices
In Druid times, human sacrifices were made to the god of the sun.

> *In the Central Highlands of Scotland bonfires, known as the Beltane fires, were formerly kindled with great ceremony on the first of May, and the traces of human sacrifices at them were particularly clear and unequivocal.*
> The Golden Bough, J.G. Frazer, abridged edn. 1922

This practice ceased but animals were sacrificed for centuries, the favourites being two white bulls.

> *The registers of the Presbytery of Dingwall for the years 1656 and 1678 contain records of the sacrifices of cattle upon the site of an ancient temple in honour of a being whom some called St Mourie, and others, perhaps knowing his doubtful character to 'ane god Mourie'.*
>
> Celtic Myth and Legend, Charles Squire, 1912

These sacrifices of cattle were meant to placate the gods and prevent plague or murrain, a cattle disease spreading through the herds.

Stones

In Bernera, 'Clachnagreine' meaning the stone of the sun and 'Clachnatrompan' – the stone of the cymbals – were connected with Beltane and Celtic worship. Music played on the Clachnatrompan was supposed to have drowned out the screams of the sacrificial victims.

Omens

Stones were placed in a circle around the ashes of the fire. People present marked them so that they could be identified. If next morning they had moved or disappeared it was a bad omen. In Druid times the entrails of the sacrificed animal, often a goat were examined and predictions were made according to what was found there.

Bannocks marked with a cross were rolled down a hill. If they broke or landed marked-side-up it signified bad luck. The yarrow was considered to be able to foretell the future. In Aberdeenshire girls gathered it, saying:

> *O it's a bonnie May mornin',*
> *I cam t'pu the yarrow;*
> *I hope before I go,*
> *To see my marrow*
>
> Traditional

Another plant supposed to be able to foretell the future was the ivy. Girls took a piece and placed it against their heart.

Ivy, ivy, I love ye,
In my bosom I put ye,
The first young lad wha speaks wi' me,
Ma marrow he will be.

Traditional

Luck

Crosses made from two sticks which had been dipped in porridge were placed over the byre for protection from fairies. This had to be carried out without anyone being seen and before sunset. These crosses were decked with flowers and carried up to the Beltane fire to be blessed before being replaced. It was unlucky to cut a blackthorn at Beltane.

Beltane bannock

Crumbs from the Beltane Bannock were gathered and sprinkled over the sheep and some were also sewn into the hem of a skirt or lining of a waistcoat, especially those of the shepherds and shepherdesses, to keep them safe from the evil eye, fairies or witches.

Plants

Rowan, ivy and bramble were made into hoops and placed beneath the milk pail to stop witches or fairies interfering with the milk, and houses were often decorated with rowan and woodbine for Beltane. The cattle being driven to the shielings were controlled with a rod made from rowan, and sheep and lambs were passed through a rowan hoop. Wells and market crosses were dressed with sacred greenery, flowers and herbs.

Food and drink

Beltane cake

As on most special occasions a special Beltane Bannock was baked. The person elected master of ceremonies brought this cake to the feast. It was covered with a sort of custard and had a scalloped edge, symbolic of the sun's rays. It was cut and everyone had a share. Sometimes trinkets were to be found in the bannock. In some places a mill-bannock with a hole in the centre was baked and the cows were milked through this hole to prevent them becoming bewitched. Pieces of this bannock were often taken by the herd lassies to the shielings to sleep on in order to foretell who would be their future husband. Another special cake was baked which had risen knobs on its surface.

> *The herds of every village hold their Beltane (a rural sacrifice). They cut a square trench in the ground, leaving the turf in the middle. On that they make a fire of wood, on which they dress a large caudle of eggs, oatmeal, butter and milk, and besides these bring plenty of beer and whisky. Each of the company must contribute something to the feast. The rites begin by pouring a little of the caudle upon the ground by way of a libation. Everyone then takes a cake of oatmeal, on which are raised nine square knobs, each dedicated to some particular being who is supposed to preserve their herds, or to some animal, the destroyer of them. Each person then turns his face to the fire, breaks off a knob, and flinging it over his shoulder, says, 'This I give to thee, O fox, spare my lambs. This I give to thee spare my eagle.'*
>
> Tour in Scotland, T. Pennant, 1769

Beltane carline

The herds enjoyed games connected with the Beltane cake whereby they were blindfolded and had to choose a piece of cake from a bonnet. One of the pieces was a sooty bannock and the person who picked it out was declared the 'Beltane Carline' or old woman. In Celtic times they would be the one to be sacrificed on the fire but later they had to leap across the flames three times and were then pelted with egg-shells.

Beltane kebbuck

Special cheeses were made for Beltane, often of sheep's milk. The wife of the house cut a piece for everyone present and placed it onto a bannock. It had to be eaten before sunset in order to keep its luck.

Beltane butter

This was butter churned before sunrise on May the first and was thought to keep the fairies away. If anyone entered while the churning was in progress they took a turn at the churn so as not to let the luck escape through the open door.

Groaning malt
This was ale made to celebrate special occasions such as births, marriages or festivals.

> *Butter, new cheise, and beir in May,*
> *Connan, cockkelis, curds and quhey.*
>
> The Evergreen, Alexander Scott, 1561

Curds and whey
In Kintyre, children had a holiday from school and visited farms to ask for their ' Maying'. This consisted of curds and cream and they threatened bad luck on any farmer's wife who would not stump up. It was a treat also taken on feast days when the townspeople would visit the country to enjoy a meal eaten out of doors. A Curd Fair was held at Kilmarnock.

Deil tak the hindmost
When the Beltane fire had been smoored and the ashes scattered, the herds raced down the hill, the last being made to look a fool. This was believed to have had a more sinister meaning in Celtic times with the one who was last becoming the next to be sacrificed.

Pipers
Before the Reformation a piper would lead the Beltane procession as it marched up the hill. After the Reformation all such celebrations were frowned on as pagan or 'Popish' and were banned in many parishes. One such famous piper was Habbie Simpson, the piper of Kilbarchan.

> *So kindly to his neighbours neast,*
> *At Beltan and Saint Barchan's feast.*
> *He blew, and then held up his briest,*
> *As he were weid*
> *But now we need not him arrest,*
> *For Habbie's deid.*
>
> Epitaph, Sir Robert Sempill of Beltrees,
> see Poems of the Sempills of Beltrees, James Patterson, 1849

Visiting wells
After St Columba brought Christianity to Scotland he blessed the sacred wells of the old religion and declared them holy. This

action was taken because the Church could not break the people's belief in the healing powers of the water drawn from these wells. St Fittock's Well, near Nigg was one of these.

> *Magrat Davidson, spouse to Andro Adam, fined £5, Scots, for sending her child to be washed at St Fiakre's [Fittoch's] Well and leaving an offering.*
>
> Minutes of the Kirk Session, Aberdour, 1630

The clootie wells on Culloden Moor and at Avoch were popular places to gather and leave offerings. These cloths must be allowed to wear away and not be removed. It was thought that the troubles of its owner would be transferred to the person who removed it. These visits took place mainly on the quarter days, including Beltane.

> *Because that the assembly of ministers and elders understood that the resort to the Dragon-Hole [Kinnoul Hill, Perth, 2nd May 1581]; as well by young men and women, with their pipes and drums striking before them through the town, had raised no small slander to this congregation, they therefore ordain that each person guilty of this practice shall pay twenty shillings to the poor, and make public repentance.*
>
> Domestic Annals of Scotland, Vol 1, From the Revolution to the Rebellion 1745, Robert Chambers, 1874

After the Reformation the General Assembly of the Church of Scotland tried to stamp out the practice by fining anyone who was found visiting a well but they were defeated and the people went on tying cloths onto trees at clootie wells, drinking three sips of the water and walking three times deasil around the well to bring luck.

MAY DAY

Floralia

Many May Day customs can be traced to the Roman Floralia. Large crowds gathered on Arthur's Seat to welcome the dawn of May Day with music and dancing around a maypole. Sick people were also carried to the top of Arthur's Seat to be exposed to the rays from the new sun as they once were in Rome.

Witchcraft

The altar in the centre was draped . . . it was a coarse white linen cloth, such as was used in the kirk at the seasons of sacrament . . . the draped altar was hidden by figures – human or infernal – moving round it in a slow dance . . . What he had taken as demons from the pit were masked mortals – one with the snout of a pig, one with a goat's horns, and the piper a gaping black hound . . . They danced widdershins against the sun . . . its slow measure became a crazy lilt, quick and furious. The piper was capering; the dancers, still going widdershins, swung round and leaped forward, flinging their limbs as in some demented reel . . . 'Oh sir, what garred ye no hearken to me and gang tae the wud on Rood-mass?'

Witchwood, John Buchan, 1924

Modern pagans

To celebrate the return of fresh growth, groups of modern pagans also meet in a clearing in a wood on May Day. They form a sacred circle and light a fire. The Lord of Winter challenges the God of the Sun to a duel with sticks. There is a Goddess of the Green Earth who blesses the cakes. Everyone drinks from a communal cup to celebrate the triumph of spring over the chaos of winter.

May blossom

In some areas it is thought to be unlucky to bring May blossom indoors but young girls gathered it and decorated the outside of their homes with it. The saying ' Ne'er cast a clout till May is oot,' meaning keep wrapped up, is perhaps referring to the appearance of the May tree blossom rather than the end of the month.

May dew

Dew was the most sacred of water to the Druids. Young girls rose early to wash their faces in the dew on May Day to ensure beauty, health and happiness.

On May Day, in a fairy ring
We've seen them round St Anton's spring,
Frae grass the caller dew-drops wring

To weet their een
And water clear as crystal spring,
To synd them clean.

Poems, Robert Fergusson, 1772

They would also gather baskets of flowers with which to dress
the May queen. May Day dew was also used to cure ailing or
weak babies and children. The mother would soak a cloth in the
dew before sunrise and then wrap the child in it to effect a cure.
Dew was also considered effective as a beauty treatment on any
quarter day.

Maypole
In the fifthteenth and sixteenth centuries in many Scottish
towns there was a festival held on May Day the centre-piece of
which was the dancing around the maypole, usually the trunk of
a tree decked with ribbons in many colours; and the occasion
also involved the crowning of a summer queen and king.

Upon the first of May, the weavers in Paul's Work, English
and Dutch set up a high Maypole, with their garlands and
bells, hanging at them, whereat was great concourse [gathering]
of people.

History of the Kirk of Scotland, David Calderwood, 1842

and

Dureing his educating in this place, [Dalserf] *they had then a*
custome every year to solemnize the first Sunday in May with
danceing about a Maypole, fyreing of pieces, and all manner
of ravelling then in use.

History of the Somerville Family, 1697

Because Dalserf was too poor to hold school sports this young
man rode to Hamilton to buy a hat, as well as a variety of
coloured ribbons to decorate it, and a pair of gloves to wear on
May Day. He also bought gunpowder for his ' fuzee', a type of
musket, so that he could take part in the shooting match at
Hamilton. A game of football was usually played on that day.

Bringing in the May
Sacred wood
In the Lowlands, especially in the cities, the branch of a tree, usually birch or rowan, was chosen, cut and dressed all over with ribbons. It was set up on a hill and everyone danced around it three times sunwise. Madge Wildfire sings:

> I am Queen of the Wake, and I'm Lady of May,
> And I lead the blithe ring round the maypole today;
>> Heart of Midlothian, Walter Scott, 1818

The original maypole was a fertility symbol to encourage the renewal of life. Arthur's Seat, Edinburgh was a favourite place for erecting one and the custom was recorded in many places up until the nineteenth century.

Edinburgh
In Edinburgh in the fifteenth and sixteenth centuries the Society of Hammermen paid a minstrel and a standard bearer to set off for the woods to carry home branches of birch to 'bring the summer into the town' while at St Andrews they appointed a summer king who was sent to the woods to hide; he was sought and captured, and brought home carried shoulder-high.

Processions
Apprentices, journeymen and master craftsmen took part in May Day processions by setting off for a day in the country dressed in their Sunday best clothes. They brought back greenery to dress the market cross.

Robin Hood games
The May game called Robin Hood was celebrated on the first Sunday in May in Glasgow and Edinburgh and other cities until the sixteenth century when it was banned along with all theatrical performances. A member of the Corporation was chosen to be Robin Hood and another as Little John, his squire; these men could pass the duty on to an actor if they did not wish to appear in public in this guise but this incurred payment of a fine. The people went to a field where this pageant was enacted and games and dancing took place. There was often

drinking and wild behaviour on these occasions and under pressure from the General Assembly of the Church of Scotland to ban the pageant, an Act of Parliament was passed in 1556.

Na manner of persone be chosen Robert Hude, nor Little John, Abbot of Unreason, Queen of May, nor otherwise.
Statute of the Sixth Parliament of Queen Mary, 1556

However, in 1561, the Magistrates of Edinburgh found themselves at the mercy of the mob when they attempted to carry this out. John Knox raged against the 'rascal multitude' who were stirred up to make a 'Robin Hude' to the annoyance of the Presbyterians who complained 'which enormity [observing the Robin Hood Play] was of many years left and damned by statute and Act of Parliament; yet would they not be forbidden' and the 'profane festivities' continued until 1592 to the anger of the General Assembly.

The mob were so enraged at being disappointed in making a Robin Hood, that they rose in mutiny, seized on the City gates, comitted robberies upon strangers; and one of the ring leaders being condemned by the Magistrates to be hanged, the mob forced open the jail, set at liberty the criminal and all the prisoners and broke in pieces the gibbet erected at the Cross for executing the malefactor. They next assaulted the Magistrates who were sitting in the Council-chamber, and who fled to the Tolbooth for shelter, where the mob attacked them, battering the doors and and pouring stones through the windows.
History of Edinburgh, Hugo Arnot, 1779

Pageants
Many of the craft guilds also took part in May Day pageants in Glasgow, Dumfries, St Andrews, Perth and Edinburgh. They were thought originally to have been part of the fertility rites of the season to give energy to the crops and ensure a good harvest but latterly were an excuse for a good time.

Dancing
A form of English Morris dancing was also performed by teams of dancers. King James IV, on a visit to Perth, was taken to watch such a performance. On a floating platform of timber 'clad

about with birks' thirteen glovers took part. They wore a costume of green caps with silver strings, red ribbons, white shoes and had bells strapped to their legs and rapiers in their hands. They performed a sword dance with many difficult steps then five stood on the shoulders of another five as the remaining three pranced in and out between their legs drinking wine and breaking glasses.

> *Whilk, God be praisit, was actit and done without hurt or skaith, till any. Whilk drew us till great charges and expenses, amounting to the sum of 350 merks.*
>
> Muse's Threnodie, Vol. 2, n.d.

May Day procession to the summer shielings

It was on the first of May that the 'triall', as the procession was called, set off to the summer pastures. These could be up to twelve miles away. The sheep led off followed by the cattle, goats, horses and dogs. Sometimes it was necessary for the herds to swim part of the way. A great deal of gear had to be carried with them. The backs of the horses carried panniers laden with goods while the men also carried huge packs on their backs. The women knitted as they walked and also helped to carry the gear.

On arrival at the shielings a bonfire was lit and a feast of lamb, cheese and bannocks was eaten. Then a service was held to bless the flocks and to ask for a prosperous summer. Often a piper would lead the procession and would play for the dancing which started up after the feast and could last until dawn.

Rowan rod

A wand of rowan was always used to drive the livestock to the shieling. It was placed above the door of the bothy for good luck and to keep away the fairies.

Empire Day

This was celebrated on May the twenty-fourth. Flags were flown from all public buildings and schools would decorate their classrooms with flags of the countries which made up the British empire. The name was later changed to Commonwealth Day. School outings and picnics were popular on Empire Day. Red, white and blue was worn.

Victoria Day

The Monday nearest to May the twenty-fourth was held as a trades holiday in many parts of Scotland. It was called Victoria Day or the Queen's Birthday. In Edinburgh, Musselburgh and Portobello bonfires were lit in the streets. In 1958 the custom was prohibited by the Corporation of Edinburgh because it damaged the surface of the street and also was a fire hazard causing in that year alone forty-six calls to the fire brigade. The tradition of bonfires may have survived from those bonfires which were lit on St John's Eve.

King's Birthday

By an Act of Parliament, this day [May 29th] *was henceforth to be held as a holiday, both as the king's birthday and as the anniversary of his majesty's restoration. All over Scotland, the ordinance seems to have been heartily complied with. Everywhere there were religious services and abstinence from labour, and in most places active demonstrations of rejoicing, as beating of drums, shooting of cannon, sounding of trumpets, setting up of bonfires, and ceremonial drinking of royal healths in public places.*
Domestic Annals of Scotland, Vol 2, From the Revolution to the Rebellion 1745,
Robert Chambers,1874

Blue gowns

Certain old men were nominated as King's Bedesmen and were given the privilege of going around Scotland begging. They wore a blue cloak and a special badge of pewter to show that they had this right. They were to pray for the health of the king which no doubt they did with fervour as on his birthday they received a new cloak and a purse containing Scots shillings, one for each year of the king's age.

David Campbell, His majesty's tailor for Scotland, came to this kingdom from Jamaica, purely on design to solemnise this day [May 29th]. *He accordingly entertained at his lodgings in the Abbey His Majesty's Blue Gowns (a set of licensed beggars, corresponding to the number of the King's years, which were now fifty), and at night he kept open table, where several*

> *gentlemen were entertained, all the royal healths were drunk,*
> *and those with the illustrious name of Campbell, with the*
> *sound of trumpet and other music.*
>
> Caledonian Mercury, October 30th 1733

Linlithgow

On May the twenty-ninth, 1662, at Linlithgow, the fountain flowed with wines from France and Spain, the public came to drink the health of the king, and sweetmeats and glasses were thrown amongst the people. An arch held representations, of an old hag 'the Covenant', a Whig, and the devil, who wore a religious habit, his 'eyes turned up in a fanatic gesture'. On the pillars were drawn 'kirk-stools, roks and reels, brochans, cogs and spoons'. This arch was set on fire and copies of the Covenant were burned. At the Palace of Linlithgow there was another bonfire and the Provost and magistrates paraded through the town.

Lennoxmill

> *I am not aware whether the employees in Lennoxmill now show*
> *their loyalty by observing the Queen's Birthday, but when*
> *George the Third was king it was the correct thing for all good*
> *citizens to observe it as a holiday, and in this way to testify*
> *their loyalty. There was a treat in the evening to all Lennoxmill*
> *workers, and the firm presented the apprentices and boys with a*
> *sum of tuppence, to be expended by them at pleasure. This was*
> *spent on fireworks if loyal, or on good things if selfish, and they*
> *were treated also at the expense of the firm to a glass of toddy,*
> *if they cared to have it. Very few in those days refused either*
> *the tuppence or the glass of toddy.*
>
> The Parish of Campsie, John Cameron, 1892

WHITSUN

Debts

Those who could not pay their debts or tithes to the church were publicly cursed on Whit-Sunday.

Whitsun Monday

In Glasgow a fair was held on Whitsun Monday which was a feeing fair.

> On that evening, all the loose boys and elder blackguardism [rascally types] of the town were attracted thither, to play tricks on what were designated Jocks and Jennies who had assembled during the day for country hire. Frequently on such occasions, have we ourselves seen the mob take possession of the streets, particularly of the avenue leading to the [Stockwell] bridge, and hereafter put to the rout both Magistry and Police; while every man with a decent coat or a good hat was certain of being assailed with a dead cat or some equally filthy missile.
>
> Glasgow and Its Clubs, John Strang, 1864

Stonebickering

Another ploy was stonebickering. These pitched battles were fought using stones as ammunition and took place between the northern and southern inhabitants of Glasgow. They were held at the Bridgend of Stockwell Street and often resulted in injuries.

MIDSUMMER

Summer solstice

The longest day was a day of celebration of the powers of the sun. It was one of the main festivals of the Druids. On its eve they gathered on the hill – chiefs and priests, tribesmen and women in all their finery – to seek omens and make sacrifices to ensure a good and bountiful harvest amidst peace and prosperity. One of their main temples was Tinto Hill in Lanarkshire on which a large fire was lit for centuries on Midsummer's Eve.

Lost souls

People believed that the spirits of the dead roamed at midsummer, on the longest day, when, especially in the north, there was very little darkness. They stayed up all night feasting and dancing as they believed that noise frightened the spirits away.

JOHNSMAS

St John's Eve

Fire was meant to boost the power of the sun so fires were lit on this day. It was a celebration of the feast of the nativity of St John the Baptist and was observed by the Christian Church instead of the pagan feast of midsummer, in honour of the longest day.

Bonfires

Bonfires were lit on St John's Eve, June the twenty-fourth, three days after the summer solstice, to frighten away the fairies. The peats were cut by everyone in the community and each one had to contribute a piece of turf for the Johnsmas fire. These fires had to burn for an afternoon and evening without going out or bad luck would follow.

Durris

A custom grew up in Durris in the eighteenth century. Alexander Hogg, who became a wealthy merchant, never forgot that he had been a young herd and donated money for a bonfire on St John's Eve on the top of Cairnshee. Every young herd who helped to collect wood for it was given a silver sixpence and the honour of lighting it went to the youngest herdsman.

Camping out

In Shetland, Johnsmas was often held by the young boys who camped out in the barn on their own, preparing their food and cooking it. Every evening they collected pails of milk from the neighbours to make milgruel (a type of porridge). They lit a fire of moss which had to stay alight for a whole afternoon and evening.

Elgin

In 1580 complaints of fires being lit on St John's Eve led to the burgesses being fined and many of the craftsmen were threatened with having their licenses revoked unless they desisted from these practices. At Aberdeen the Kirk Session, in 1608, complained of fires being lit in front of houses.

Luck

The people danced around the fires and in some places leapt over the flames for luck. Heather was collected for several days and made into besoms which were lit from the fire and carried around the boundaries for luck. Farmers also used to carry lit heather besoms around their cattle three times sunwise for protection from illness.

Animal bone

In Orkney a bone was thrown into the bonfire on St John's Eve for protection of the animals from supernatural interference. This was a relic of the animal sacrifice of the Druids.

Johnsmas flowers
Divination

Not to be outdone, the girls held a 'banquet' to lay up the Johnsmas flowers. They searched the countryside for ribwort plantain and selected two stalks, one shorter than the other. These represented the girl and her possible sweetheart. From these the florets were removed before they were rolled in a docken leaf and buried in the ground. If next morning the florets had reappeared on one, it was a sign of hope and if on both, an indication of certain happiness.

Decoration

On St John's Eve greenery, especially birch, was brought into the house and placed over doorways to give protection from the fairies. Many people stayed awake all night because they were afraid that if they fell asleep their soul would leave their body and hover over the place where they would eventually meet their death.

Plants

Herbs were considered to be at their most powerful on St John's Eve and were often gathered then for drying so that their properties would be preserved. The petals of the rose, vervain, St John's Wort and trefoil were carefully picked as these were thought to be sacred plants which gave protection from evil as well as having healing powers.

Fernseed

It was believed that if the seed of the fern was caught as it fell to the ground on the Eve of St John the person catching it could become invisible at will.

Peat

Pieces of burnt peat were collected by the girls who carried them home and dipped them in urine from the byre. They placed these above the door of their house and left them overnight. Next morning the fibres were examined for the colour of the hair of the lad they would marry.

Scrofula

> *This day being St John's Day, the king* [Charles I] *went in state to the Chapel Royal, Holyroodhouse, and there, after a solemn offertory, touched about a hundred persons for the king's evil,* [scrofula], *putting about their necks a piece of gold, coined for the purpose, hung at a white silk riband.*
>
> Domestic Annals of Scotland, Vol 2, From the Revolution to the Rebellion 1745,
> Robert Chambers, 1874

Petermas

This was held, especially in the Hebrides, on June the twenty-ninth. Fires were lit in front of the houses and fish-oil was burned in a cruzie. It had to burn away completely to bring luck. There were tables placed out of doors and neighbours were invited to eat and drink with the family. A sort of first-footing took place. At Glass, in 1608, the Kirk Session complained of midsummer fires being lit on St Peter's Eve.

Straw wheel

A wheel of covered in straw was set alight and rolled down the hill to carry away any ill-luck.

Martin Bullion Day

This was held on July the fourth, old style or the fifteenth, new style. It was also known as Bulgan Day and in Buchan as Marcabillin's Day. It was considered a good sign if the deer rose dry and lay down dry on Martin Bullion Day. It corresponded to St Swithin's Day in England and if it rained the weather forecast would be rain for a further forty days and nights.

Autumn

LAMMAS

*T*he Celtic feast of Lugh was held on August the first and was called Lugnasaid. This is often thought to be the origin of Lammas, a quarter day in Scotland. However another explanation is given which reckons the name to be a corruption of 'Loafmas', as the day on which a loaf of bread was baked from the first fruits of the harvest season. Many fairs were held then as it was a holiday for farmfolk.

> *Even the herds had a half-holiday; in anticipation of which they carefully kept their cows off a piece of grass long in advance of the fair (and hence called a Lammas bite) so that on the morning of it the animals were turned into the reserve pasture which would furnish them as much grass in a forenoon as they could get the whole day under ordinary circumstances.*
>
> Reminiscences, J. Simson, 1882

Lammas towers
All the herds in a district, towards the begining of summer, gathered in bands of up to one hundred herds. Each community agreed to build a tower near the centre of their district at which they would all meet at Lammas, August the first. It was usually

about four feet square and built by piling sods of earth on top
of each other, tapering towards the top like a pyramid. It would
stand about seven or eight foot high. They then placed a
flagpole in the centre and hoisted a flag bussed with ribbons. In
some places these were later converted into stone towers.

Lammas table
Two ditches about two feet deep were cut leaving a centre-piece
two feet wide topped with green divots. This made table and
chairs for the herds on which they ate their Lammas feast. They
shared the bannocks and cheese with poor or orphan boys.
Games were played and races run.

Lammas brother or sister
At Kirkwall, Orkney, at Lammas young people paired off for
the period of the Lammas fair when they were known as
Lammas brothers and sisters.

Handfasting
Lammas was a favourite time for selecting a partner to live with
for a year. If after this time the couple decided not to marry they
could go their own ways without any stigma being attached to
the woman. If a child was conceived within the year it became
the responsibility of the father. Many couples were married the
next year either over the blacksmith's anvil or by a wandering
priest, often known as a 'Book in the Bosum' priest.

Horses
It was customary to take horses for a swim in the sea at
Lammas. This may have been because at that season the water
would be warmer after the summer sun had shone on it. The
origin of the custom is pagan and was frowned on by the kirk.

> *That non goe to Leith on Lambmesday nor tak their horses to be*
> *washed in the sea.*
>   Kirk Session Records, Parish of St Cuthbert's, 16 – –

Bonfires
These were lit at Lammas, as on most quarter days to keep away
the evil spirits. The custom was continued in Ayrshire until the
late nineteenth century where the 'Tannel' was lit on the Eve of

Lammas. A piper danced a reel around it and fuel was collected by herds for several weeks before it.

Bannocks
Bonnach Lunas or Lammas bannock was specially baked for Lammas as for all quarter days. The Luineag was the name of an individual bannock baked for a female and Luinean the one for a male.

MARYMAS

At Marymas, held on August the fifteenth, originally in honour of the Virgin Mary, a bannock was toasted in front of a fire of sacred wood. This was divided between the members of the family. The father carried the embers of the fire in an iron pot while each member carried their piece of bannock as they walked three times deasil or sunwise around their house to protect it from the evil eye and the fairies.

The fatling of Mary
Early on the morning of the Festival of Mary the Great, in the Western Isles, ears of corn were picked to make bere-meal. The ears were laid out on a rock to dry, then husked by hand and winnowed in a fan before being ground in the quern. They were then kneaded on a sheepskin, and formed into a bannock which was called the fatling of Mary.

FEAST OF ST BARR

September the twenty-seventh was known as the Feast of St Barr and was celebrated on Barra.

> All the inhabitants observe the anniversary of St Barr, being the 27th September; it is performed riding on horseback, and the solemnity is concluded by three turns round St Barr's church.
> A Description of The Western Isles, Martin Martin, 1703

MICHAELMAS

The Festival of St Michael was celebrated on September the twenty-ninth. Michael was the patron saint of the sea and sailors, which made his a very important festival in the West of Scotland.

Carrot Sunday

The Sunday afternoon before the festival the women and girls would go to the fields and pull carrots. When a forked carrot was found a shout went up as this was considered very good fortune.

> Little cleft one! little cleft one!
> Joy of carrot surpassing to me!
> Little cleft one! little cleft one!
> Fruitage of carrot surpassing to me!
>
> Michael militant will give me seed and fruit,
> Calm Brigit will give me passion
> Fite Fith will give me wine and milk,
> And Mary mild will give me aid.

Traditional

The carrots were taken home and the earth washed off them before they were put into bunches which were tied with red thread and stored in pits, covered with sand until they were required. The bunches were of the circumference of the thumb and forefinger joining at the tips. The carrot was a fertility symbol. It was always given by a woman to a man.

Michaelmas Eve

Michael's cake

Fires of oak, rowan or bramble were lit in the houses in readiness for baking the Struan Michael or Michael's cake. It was made from the oats, bere and rye which was grown throughout the year. The meal was moistened with milk from sheep and was baked on a lambskin by the eldest daughter of the family who would croon as she baked it:

> Progeny and prosperity of family,
> Mystery of Michael, protection of Trinity.

Traditional

A batter of butter, eggs and cream was pasted onto the layers as it baked with the tail feathers of a cockerel. Fruit, honey and caraway seeds were also added to the mixture. Other larger communal cakes were also baked and little individual cakes were made for every member of the family including those absent or having died during the year. These latter were given to the poor.

Ill-luck

If the cake broke while being baked something terrible would happen to the baker and if it broke after firing but before the time for it to be eaten then ill-luck would come to the family. The broken cake was never used.

Animals

The crumbs were placed into a footless stocking and taken and swung over the sheep in the field on St Michael's Day to protect them from evil spirits. In Uist a piece of dough, called the Devil's dough, was toasted then thrown over the left shoulder and the devil told to stay away from the baker's cattle. A similar custom was called the fox's bit and was supposed to keep the fox from the hens. On St Kilda on Michaelmas Eve at the area known as the Plain of Spells the beasts were 'sained' – washed and blessed with salt and water and driven through fire for protection against the evil eye.

Lamb

One or more lambs were killed for the feasting the next day for each family. They had to be male and have no spot or blemish. A quarter of the lamb was given with a peck of meal, a quarter of bannock, a quarter of cheese and some butter to the poor and to orphans.

Horses

The men set up guard parties to watch for anyone removing their horses. It was customary to borrow a horse to ride in the St Michael's Cavalcade the next day. At least one horse had to be left for the owner to ride. The borrowed horse was ridden until the race then it was returned to its owner.

St Michael's Day
Bannocks

In Barra the bannock was baked and eaten on St Michael's Day and everyone present in the house, whether family or stranger, had to eat a piece of it. It was baked originally with the meal from the first grain ground that year. Later scones were made with flour and treacle or currants and caraway seeds.

Blessings

The struans were taken with care to the church to be blessed early on St Michael's Day. There was a service of thanksgiving for a good harvest. Families returned home to eat the cakes. This was done with ceremony. The father placed it on a well scrubbed board and used a knife:

> *Without stain, without dust,*
> *Without smear, without flaw,*
> *Without grime, without rust.*
> Traditional

He made the sign of the cross then cut it into small portions. He then carved the lamb also into small pieces. The family members all took a piece of the cake in their left hand and a bit of lamb in their right and sang a hymn in praise of St Michael thanking him for all their blessings. The father and mother then took their gifts to the poor.

Cavalcade

The pilgrimage or St Michael's Cavalcade was undertaken by everyone except the very old and the babies. The horses were mounted in twos, each wife sitting on horseback behind her husband. Sisters sat behind brothers, little brothers in front of big ones, young women sat behind their sweethearts. Everyone wore their best clothes and set out to make their pilgrimage to the Chapel of the titular saint. They went deasil around the burying ground led by the priests, also on horseback, and followed by other people who were on foot. The person sitting behind gave a handful of carrots to the one in front at the end of the round of their forefathers' graves to wish them peace and prosperity.

Oda

This is the name given to the games and races after the cavalcade. It included tests of athletic skill, foot-races and horse-races. St Michael was the patron saint of horses.

Horse races
These were held on a long, firm stretch of sandy beach. The riders went bare-headed and bare-foot, wearing only a shirt and trews. They raced without a saddle and bridle keeping their horses in order with lengths of sea-tangle. Some girls competed in a ladies-race.

Dancing
In every area a dance was held in the largest house. Pipers took turns at playing and every man paid a sixpence for the piper, if he was a married man, otherwise he played free. Specific dances existed which were traditionally performed on this day. These may have dated back to the Druids as wands were used. The man touched the head of the woman with the wand and she fell down, as though dead. He grieved over her then breathed on the palm of her hand and sole of her foot to bring her to life. He then touched her heart with the wand and she regained her energy. The two then danced frantically to mouth music. Other dances such as the sword-dance, the *'seann triubhas'* and the Reel of Tulloch were also popular.

Gifts
Gifts were exchanged after the cavalcade or at the dances held in the evening.

> *Girls gave the men bonnets, hose, garters, cravats, purses or plaids while the men in return gave brooches of silver, brass or copper, knives, scissors, snoods, combs or mirrors.*
> Carmina Gadelica, Alexander Carmichael, 1899

Gifts of a struan were also made by the wives of the farmworkers to their land superior as a token of goodwill. The land superior, whether clan chief, laird or proprietor, joined in the festival and attended the games and dances.

Carrots
The women and girls filled white linen bags which had an identification on them with carrots. These they took with them to the dance. The carrots were hidden near the house where the dancing was to take place. From time to time they brought a bunch into the dance.

It is I that have the carrots,
Whoever he be that can take them from me.

Traditional

The carrots were symbols of progeny and prosperity, triumph and increase, fame and fortune until the day of death and after it.

LUKEMAS

Sour Cakes Day

St Luke's Day, held on October the eighteenth, was often known as Sour Cakes Day. It was especially celebrated in the Royal Burgh of Rutherglen and there was a great deal of ritual connected with it.

Baking the bannock

At sunset on St Luke's Eve a line was chalked on the floor of the house of the woman chosen as the Queen, the Bride or the Toaster. She sat with her six or seven 'maidens' within this line which onlookers must not cross as it was considered consecrated ground. If they should break this rule they had to provide drink for the company. The rites had echoes of paganism. The women sat on the ground in a circular formation with their feet facing towards the fire. The Queen sat beside the fire with a bowl of leavened dough which was prepared about ten days previously and left to ferment. The woman next to the fire on the east side was called the Todler and the one on the west – the Hodler. The others are given fun names such as Mistress Baker or the Worst Maid.

Each 'maiden' had a large wooden baking board. Dough was brought out and rolled into balls which were covered in aniseed and sugar. The Todler took a ball and formed it into a cake which she placed on the board of the Hodler. She beat it a little thinner and passed it around the circle of women from east to west, deasil or sunwise. Each woman beat the cake until it was wafer thin, when it was given back to the Toaster, who fired it on the girdle hung over the open fire. It was usual for a song to be sung to give a rhythmic beat to the work. There was laughter and joking as the cakes were baked. They were then given away as presents at St Luke's Fair. It is possible that this ceremony, especially as it had to be carried out with such detail, was a survival of the baking of cakes to pacify the Queen of Heaven in the ancient cult of moon worship.

Sour cream

Another custom was the making of sour cream which was a speciality of the area. It was prepared in a wooden vessel and covered by a linen cloth. When separated the whig or whey was drawn off from the bottom by releasing a bung. The remainder was beaten with a wooden spoon until whipped. This was then eaten with the cakes.

Dram and cakes

> *We have ourselves witnessed this curious operation in the Thistle Inn of Rutherglen within the past two or three years. This mystic baking requires for its proper execution the services of six or eight elderly ladies . . . These cakes, which we have often tasted . . . are like a wafer in thickness, of an agreeable aciduous taste, and lend an additional relish to the drams usually in extra demand at this time.*
>
> *Rambles around Glasgow,* Hugh MacDonald, 1854

At Sanquhar on Lukemas Day men wore women's clothing and the horns of oxen and ran through the streets.

BATTER-DOOR-NIGHT

This was held the night before Hallowe'en in Elgin. Boys would pull stalks of kail leaving the root attached and run through the streets hitting the house doors with it. In Caithness and Sutherland it was the garden gates and farm gates which were removed. Sometimes these were floated down the river. Another ploy was to exchange animals, a black horse for a white. The owners were left to sort out this mischief the next day. This compares with Mischief Night, held on November the fourth in many parts of England.

HALLOWMAS

This was the celebration of the beginning of winter known in the time of the Druids as *'Samhain'*, a corruption of *'Sainfuin' – sain* (summer) and *fuin* (ending) = summer's end.

Originally the Romans celebrated their Ferralia, in February. They visited the graves of their relatives to offer up prayers and sacrifices were made at bonfires. In 993 A.D. the Christian Church decided to change this to November the second and converted it into All Souls Day.

The Druids were supposed to believe that the Lord of Death gathered all the spirits of the dead who had been made to enter the bodies of animals as punishment for their sins and redistributed them, on Hallowe'en, the last day of the Celtic year.

It was also believed that the spirits of the dead came back to their old haunts at this time. Fires were lit to guide them home and to frighten away evil spirits. The dead were offered food and drink – a custom now followed by children guising. The Christian Church then named this All Hallow's Eve and the day following, All Saints Day but the old customs remained. These often conjured up witches and ghosts in the minds of those participating and unnerved the more sensitive souls who, carried away by their own imagination, told amazing tales of what they thought they had seen. It was a chance for the mischievous to play tricks.

Hallowe'en, the poem by Robert Burns, gives a vivid description of the majority of the rites which were common to most of Scotland on that bewitching night. Under pressure from the kirk elders of the Church of Scotland men were punished by the kirk for dressing up or taking part in some of the divination rituals and through time these customs were abandoned and left, in a watered-down fashion, for the children to carry on.

Bonfires
Fire of Peace
The original fire which was lit by friction, using no metal, was a fire for sacrifices to the sun god as a thanksgiving for a good harvest. It was called the fire of peace.

Home fires
At one time, as recorded in Glenlyon in 1882, every house lit its own bonfire in front of the door. Bracken or heather torches were lit from this fire and the family walked in procession –

headed by the father, mother, and each child in order of age plus any other relatives living there – three times sunwise around the house, carrying this torch in their right hand, to protect the house and family, including the livestock, from the evil eye, illness or death. After this they threw the torches into a heap and started a bonfire around which they danced. Queen Victoria took part in this ceremony at Balmoral.

Boundaries
A farmer sometimes accompanied by his herds would circle the boundaries of each field to ensure prosperity for the oncoming year. This was a throw-back to the calendar of the Druids who considered that Samhain was the first day of the new year.

Paisley
In Paisley boys built bonfires on pockets of land in the little 'islands' in the middle of the White Cart River to chase away the witches.

Ashes
Herds, waiting to be fee'd at the Martinmas fairs, sang a traditional song on All Hallow's Day as as they scattered the ashes of the Hallowe'en fire.

This is Hallaeven
The morn is Halladay
Nine free nichts till Martinmas
As soon they'll wear away.
Traditional

Ristin' the Hallow fire
Stones were buried in the ashes of the fire. These were marked, as on other occasions, so that they could be identified by their owners. When the fire was smoored the stones were examined for omens.

Wild behaviour
The young farmworkers, often through too much drink, became wild and enjoyed leaping over the fire and chasing each other with the lighted brands. However, on occasions, there were complaints that they did damage to property with their wild behaviour, setting stooks on fire and scattering them about.

*The old customs . . . have now become almost obsolete, and
the sooner they disappear altogether the better it will be for
the peace of the community in general, if what took place in
Campbeltown on Tuesday night is a specimen of the proper
thing to do on such occasions. A noisy band of youths ran
howling and screaming through the quieter streets, smashing
every door they came to with sticks and stones, whereby the
peaceably disposed inhabitants were very considerably alarmed
and disturbed.*

Campbeltown Courier, November 1882

Black Mass

There were supernatural associations with Hallowe'en. It was
thought to be the most dangerous time when a crack would
appear between this world and the other-world.

*Further on there stands a kirk, sinister and grim
Like the empty shell of man when life is leaving him.
Shadows hover in the porch and the place is cursed;
By the door an image hangs, a crucifix reversed.
Cobwebs drape the rotting pews; thick upon the wall
Whispering bats and spiders swing; sleepy blowflies crawl.
Fear and silence fill the church, such as ghosts inspire -
Yes, I swear that something moved in the darkness by the choir.*

*Close to the crumbling altar rail the grisly figure stands
And holds a book in shadow claws that once were human hands,
The pews are filled with crouching men, lit by the ragged moon,
The organ groans an anthem dim, a tune that is no tune.
Far through the night a human cry echoes in terror wild;
The cry is of an aged man, it issues from a child,
And down the aisle six votaries in slow procession stalk;
Their foot is silent and they leave no footstep as they walk . . .*

Legends of the Scottish Borders, Francis Merrilees, 1947

Turnips

Turnips have always featured at Hallowe'en, possibly because
of their availablility. In the United States of America the
pumpkin serves the same purpose.

Lanterns
The inside of a turnip is scooped out until only the thinnest skin is left. Two eyes, a nose and a mouth are cut out to make a face as gruesome as possible. Straw or twine is placed on either side of the face to make a handle for carrying it. A small candle is placed at the bottom and, when lit, it gives a yellow glow to frighten away the evil spirits. Ghouls, goblins and strange beasties were believed to move around freely that night.

Wands
In Lewis, the boys carried turnips and cut wands from rowan. They challenged each other to a fight – the winner was the one who snatched away the turnip.

Masks
A false face, usually depicting a ghost, devil or witch, was originally worn so that the real identity would be hidden and the person would blend in with the evil spirits who were abroad; This allowed the adult, as this was an adult festival in the past and not only for children, to roam the streets or cross the fields unmolested by the spirits.

Animals
Mare-stanes
These were rough hatchet-shaped stones found in rivers, usually worn down by friction. They were hung up in the stable on Hallowe'en to prevent the horses from being ridden by an old hag, a witch called The Mare.

Food and drink
Fruit and nuts
The use of fruits and nuts comes from the Roman Festival of 'Pomona', dedicated to the goddess of fruit trees. These, especially apples, chestnuts and peanuts, are still popular at Hallowe'en.

Dooking (Ducking) for apples
The apples were placed in a basin of water and each person in turn tried to lift one out with their teeth or else drop a fork from their mouth to spear an apple as the fruit was stirred round to make the task more difficult. This was usually done kneeling over the back of a wooden chair.

Tatties and neeps

The turnip, removed from the inside of its skin, is boiled and pepper and salt and butter are mixed in as it is mashed. It is served with mashed potatoes. At one time trinkets were hidden in the mixture.

Stovies

This potato dish was always a favourite. It is potatoes cooked with onions, usually in dripping and in some places pieces of meat or sausages are added. Trinkets were often put into this mixture.

Cheese pudding

A sort of soufflé made with eggs, bread, cheese and milk.

Broken bannocks and blessings

It was considered very bad luck if an oatcake or bannock should break on a saint's day. The left-over meal was placed in a stocking and sprinkled over the sheep with a blessing to protect them against the evil eye.

Treacle scones

These scones or even pancakes spread with treacle were hung from a beam or pulley by a cord and everyone had to try to take a bite as it was swung.

Divination
Salted herring

In Lewis it was customary to eat salted herring on Hallowe'en in the hope that a future spouse would appear that night in a dream.

Hot lead

Molten lead was dropped through the hole at the top of a key and whatever shape it made was interpreted to be a tool of the trade of a future spouse.

Straws

Two straws were stood upright in the ashes of the fire. They were named for a couple. If they burned at the same pace the couple would marry and live in harmony. If not, their marriage would be stormy.

Lucky dip

A bowl of oatmeal and cream was made and the girl rolled up her sleeve and plunged in her hand hoping to find a trinket – a thimble, ring, button or silver threepenny. Eggs, apples, nuts, bowls filled with water and soot, and even herring fat were used to discover a future spouse.

Harrows

Three harrows were lined up outside a barn at midnight. One young man was blindfolded and passed back and forth through the harrows then pushed through the barn window. He waited there alone and on hearing a noise or a voice he removed the blindfold. He must never reveal what he saw or heard or he would die.

Kail stocks

The company set off for a field where they were blindfolded and moved across as they pulled kail stalks. These were pulled after dark. If the stalk was crooked or straight, long or short this would be the stature of their future spouse. Sometimes a lad and lass who were courting held hands and pulled a kail stalk together. If it had plenty of good rich earth around its roots their future would be prosperous.

Oat stalks

Girls would gather oat stalks and count the number of seeds to find out how many children they would bear. Each seed equalled a child.

Blue clue

After a ritual selection by the time honoured 'you are out' rhyme or by drawing the short straw, a girl was chosen to go alone to a dark, lonely corn kiln, climb to the upper ridge of the kiln-logie, and wait there in darkness. The girl let down a long thread and asked, 'Wha hauds?' The answer was supposed to be the name of her future spouse.

> *She thro' the yard the nearest taks,*
> *An' to the kiln she goes then,*
> *An' darklins grapit for the bauks,*
> *And in the blue clue throws then,*

Right fear't that night.
An' ay she win't, an ay she swat,
I wat she made nae jaukin;
Till something held within the pat,
Guid Lord! but she was quaukin!
But whether 'twas the Deil himsel,
Or whether 'twas a bauk-en',
Or whether it was Andrew Bell,
She did na wait on talkin
To speir that night.

Hallowe'en, Robert Burns, 1786

Nuts

Sweethearts placed a pair of nuts on the fire. If they burned quietly they would have a happy marriage but if they sparked it would be a fiery one. Boys, in Galloway, collected wrack-boxes which clung to seaweed. They would add a peat to the fire, especially if the nuts were for their brother or sister, and underneath it they placed these boxes. When they exploded the unfortunate couple believed that it was the nuts and that their union was doomed until they were let into the secret.

Tricks

Doors were battered with kail-stalks and window rapping was practised as well as more inconvenient tricks such as placing a divot on a chimney which made the smoke blow back into the house. Hollow stalks of seawrack were also used to blow smoke through letter boxes of houses in the nineteenth century.

Witches

In Scotland in the sixteenth and seventeenth centuries, witches were not vague supernatural beings. Intelligent and educated people, including ministers of the Church of Scotland, believed implicitly in their existence and that they were minions of the Devil. Many women and a few men were put to death for imagined deeds. The Hallowe'en witch, however, was older than these and was synonymous with the Blue Hag of Winter. St Bride held sway throughout the spring and summer months but in autumn she was overcome by the old 'Cailleach' who devastated the land and who imprisoned her within Ben Nevis.

It is this traditional witch with her black cat and broomstick who appears on cakes and decorations and whom children impersonate at fancy-dress parties.

> *Fun and frolic still are rampant,*
> *Lanterns, guisers, aye are seen;*
> *Baith in country and in city,*
> *There's honour paid to Hallowe'en*
>
> *Melodies and Memories,* John Black, 1909

All Souls' Day

This was the day on which prayers were offered for the souls of the dead. In 998 AD it was decreed that it be held on November the second. Alms were always given to the poor but they had to ask for them.

Fireworks

Bonfires and fireworks are a fairly recent celebration on November the fifth. In Scotland it was usually effigies of the radicals Thomas Paine or Wilkes that were burned and not Guy Fawkes, even though the news of the discovery of the Gun-Powder Plot, in 1605, was received with rejoicing in Scotland.

> *At this time, too, it was customary for the schoolboys on the anniversary of the Gunpowder Plot, to burn Wilkes, instead of as formerely, Guy Fawkes. An effigy of Wilkes was kept suspended all day near a large fire, while certain of the band of boys which surrounded it collected money from passengers at the houses. Towards dusk the stock was divided among the juvenile fraternity, after which the effigy was paraded; and having placidly suffered all manner of indignities, it underwent the ordeal of being consumed in the fire, amid the shouts and huzzas of the spectators.*
>
> *Glasgow and Its Clubs,* John Strang, 1864

MARTINMAS

The Feast of St Martin was held on November the eleventh, one of the Scottish quarter days. It is usually referred to as Martinmas but often pronounced Martimas. It was the same

day as Hallowe'en in the old calendar. In the tradtitional ballad
the 'Wife of Usher's Well', her sons return from the dead.

> *It fell about the Martinmas,*
> *When nights are lang and mirk,*
> *The carlin's wife's three sons came hame,*
> *And their hats were made o' the birk.*
> *It neither grew in syke nor ditch,*
> *Nor yet in ony sheugh,*
> *But at the gates o' Paradise,*
> *The birk grew fair eneugh.*
>
> Traditional

At cock crow the spirits would return to their graves. The
crowing of a cockerel, especially a black one, was also thought
to frighten away evil spirits.

Mart

Fodder was scarce in the days before the Agricultural Revolution
of the mid-seventeenth century and in the eighteenth century
the approach to crop husbandry changed. Oxen were killed and
butchered and salted to preserve the meat which was used over
the winter as food. These were called marts.

Haggis

This was always a popular dish at Martinmas. The entrails of
the animals which were slaughtered were mixed with oatmeal
and stuffed into a sheep's bladder to be boiled. Spices were
added to help to preserve them. Another favourite which used
up the blood was black puddings. White mealy puddings were
also popular.

ANERMAS

St Andrew

St Andrew was adopted as the patron saint of Scotland after a
famous Pictish Victory in 747 A.D. in the reign of Aengus. A
huge saltire was seen in the sky which they believed turned the
tide in their favour. His relics were believed to be housed at
St Andrews. It is a day more celebrated abroad by ex-patriots
than in Scotland.

King James IV celebrated it by a Saint Andrew's Dinner.

And ilka year for his patron's saik,
Ane banquet royall wald he maik,
With wild fowle, venisoun and wyne.

Squire Meldrum, David Lyndsay, 1879

Sanct Andra-ing

Traps were set for rabbits and squirrels and the farmworkers set off to the woods on what was known as 'going Sanct Andra-ing'. They brought these home to be cooked and there was feasting and drinking.

Observance

There was also a kind of volunteer effort in certain classes to get up an observance of the day consecrated to the national saint, November 30th, 1662, a Sunday. Many of our nobles, barons, gentry and others of the Kingdom put on ane livery or favour of revenue therof. This being a novelty I thought good to record it, because it was never of use herto fore since the Reformation.

Domestic Annals of Scotland, Vol 2, From the Revolution to the Rebellion 1745, Robert Chambers, 1874

International

There are St Andrew's societies in many parts of the world which hold dinners on the night of November the thirtieth. They wear tartan, the kilt, sing Scots songs and dance Scottish reels and strathspeys.

The scattered clans are ane this nicht,
Nae mair we war wi' ane anither,
'Auld Scotland Yet!' for Scotland's richt
We'll bide the warld's fueds the-gither.

Sanct Andrew's Nicht, George Leith, n d.

The Saltire

The saltire of St Andrew, a white diagonal cross on a deep blue background, is the national flag of Scotland and is flown from all public buildings. It was incorporated into the Union Flag after the Act of Union of Parliaments in Scotland and England in 1707.

Winter

YULE

Yule was the name given to a period of time during December
and January. It usually began with the shortest day and ended
on Twelfth Night or Uphalieday. The name derives from the sun
and it is a sun festival although held in the midst of winter.

When merry Yule-day comes, I trow,
You'll scantlin find a hungry mou;
Sma' are our cares, our stamacks fou
O' gusty gear
And kickshaws, strangers to our view,
Sin fairn-year.

Ye browster wives now busk ye bra',
An' fling your sorrows far awa';
Then come and gies the tither blaw
Of reaming ale,
Mair precious than the well of Spa,
Our hearts to heal . . .
Fidlers, your pins in temper fix,
And roset weel your fiddlesticks,
But banish vile Italian tricks

From out your quorum,
Nor fortes wi' pianos mix,
Gie's Tulloch Gorum

The Daft Days, Robert Fergusson, 1772

Auld Yule

The original date of Yule in the Julian Calendar which was in use before 1752 placed it on January the fifth. There were riots when the calendar was altered and many people refused to hold Christmas on the new date of December the twenty-fifth. For several years there were celebrations of New Christmas and Old Christmas which led to a mixture of similar customs taking place on both dates. In some places, especially in Shetland, Auld Yule, January the fifth, was still maintained up until the Second World War.

All Heal

The Druids also held a festival at the time of the winter solstice, December the twenty-first and called it *'Nuadhulig'*, New All-Heal or new mistletoe. The people went to the forests to join the priests in search of mistletoe growing on an oak tree. The priest climbed the tree and cut the mistletoe with a golden knife. It fell onto a cloth of white linen. At the spot where it was found two white bulls were sacrificed. At one time humans were also sacrificed. The plant was carefully carried home. There was a religious service followed by feasting, singing and dancing and the next day the mistletoe was divided amongst the people who hung it up in their houses or above their doors to ward off evil and to give the fairies a shelter from the frost. This was considered the first day of the year.

Saturnalia

The Roman festival at the winter solstice was known as Saturnalia and lasted for seven days in honour of Saturnus, known also as the Sower. It was a feast of celebration for the fruits of the earth and hope for their renewal. Bacchus, the god of wine, played a major part in this festival. Many of the rites and customs have survived in the form of giving, decorating a tree with lights, of paper hats, balloons and the blowing of paper trumpets. Pantomime is a survival of the masquerades and the complete turning upside-down of the right order of things.

YULE BANNED

After the Reformation attempts were made to ban the celebration of Yule. No holiday was permitted.

26th November 1649
The said day, the minister and elders being convened in session,
and after invocation in the name of God, intimate that Yule
be not kept, but that they yoke their oxen and horse, and
employ their servants in their service that day as well as on
other work days.

Kirk Session Records, Parish of Slains, 1649

This was upheld by the General Assembly of the Church of Scotland and, although still defied by many people, led to Christmas Day being a working day up until the 1960s.

This Christmas Day [1574] *the minister and reader of Dumfries*
having refused to teach or read, the Town . . . brought a reader
of their own, with tabret [drum] *and whistle, and caused him to*
read the prayers – this extraordinary exercise they maintained
all the days of Yule.

Domestic Annals of Scotland, Vol 1, From the Revolution to the Rebellion 1745,
Robert Chambers, 1874

Up until the 1970s many older people did not open any presents which they received at Christmas until New Year's Day

CHRISTMAS

Daft Days

These were the days at Yule, covering Christmas and New Year when the opportunity for a great deal of merriment was welcomed as a break during the long dark days of winter. Neighbours visited each other and friends from afar, or family who had moved away returned home. At one time ghost stories and tales of the supernatural were told around the fire and there was singing of favourite songs.

Daft Friday
A ball is held at the University of Glasgow on the last Friday of the Christmas term. This lasts until breakfast the following morning.

St Thomas Day
The Christian Church declared December the twenty-first as the Feast of St Thomas the Apostle. On that day the poor could ask for alms and were often given food to help them enjoy the season of Yule. In return they sometimes gave the giver a sprig of holly. In Shetland children joined in and it was an excuse for guising on Thomasmas. In Renfrewshire in 1839 a private diary records that they set out in droves between five and six o'clock to seek their Yule bannocks.

Yule holidays
School holidays began on December the twenty-first and lasted until January the eleventh in pre-Reformation times. This changed, and as late as 1928 some schools did not go on holiday until New Year. In 1642 it fell on a Sunday and in Aberdeen the people were warned not to take part in superstitious practices. However the Church of Scotland was less worried about such practices and more afraid that those of the Roman Church would prevail and it was for that reason that they shunned Christmas for so long.

Barring-out Day
This was the name given in many areas to December the twenty-first. The pupils closed the doors or made a barrier at the gates of the school and kept out the masters until they agreed to grant them a holiday.

Aberdeen
In the sixteenth century, the boys of the Grammar School took possession of their school and barred the masters until they agreed to give them a fortnight's holiday. Again, at Yule, in 1604, the boys were accused of

> *Keeping and halding the same against their masters with swords, guns, pistols, and other weapons, spulying and taking puir folks*

geir, sic as geese, fowls, peats, and other vivres, during the halding therof.

Domestic Annals of Scotland, Vol 1, From the Revolution to the Rebellion 1745, Robert. Chambers, 1874

Preparations

Yule-stack

As many peats as would last a household over the thirteen days of Yule were gathered and made into a yule-stack. The fodder and bedding for the animals was also prepared and was called Yule-straw.

Officer's Corn

This was the name given to a gratuity or tithe which was paid in oatmeal to the baron court-officer of the Burgh of Barony at Yuletide.

> *Forsyth used a half firlot for receiving his officer's corn or Yule-bannock, different from the measure commonly used in that country* [Scotland].
>
> Punishment of Crimes, D. Hume, 1714

CHRISTMAS EVE

Divination

As on most special occasions Christmas Eve was seen as an opportunity to have fortunes read. Bannocks were baked on the girdle and every unmarried person present had their fortune told by choosing an egg and dropping it into a glass. The shape which was formed by the white foretold the occupation of a future spouse. The eggs, with oatmeal and milk, were then used to bake the cake. The cake was also marked so that it could be identified. It was bad luck if the cake should break during firing.

Yule-fee

This was a payment made to a Town Official, especially the Town Drummer or minstrel at Christmas. It began to die out in the early nineteenth century. Yule-wages were bonuses given to workers at Christmas, usually on Christmas Eve. In the north of Scotland merchants gave yule-candles to their customers and for many years, up until the Second World War, grocers and other merchants gave caddies of tea and calendars to their regular customers.

Christmas Old Wife

The 'Cailleach Nollaigh', Christmas Old Wife or 'Yeel-Carlin' were names given to a stump of a tree which the head of the household carved out from a piece of wood, preferably oak, in the shape of an old woman. He went to the woods to select it on Christmas Eve and hauled it home. It represented cold and death and was thrown on to the fire on Christmas Eve where it had to burn until it was reduced to ashes so that death would bypass the house during the coming year.

Rowan

The burning of rowan at Christmas was a sign of the burning away of any mistrust and jealousy between family, friends or neighbours during Yuletide.

Food and drink
Yule-bread

This was unleavened bread and more of a bannock. In some areas it was traditionally baked on Christmas Eve between noon and six o'clock. In others, such as in Banff in the nineteenth century, it must be baked between eight and nine o'clock on Christmas Eve over the Yeel Carlin. In some places individual bannocks were baked for each member of the family and the one who found a trinket would have good luck and prosper.

Yule-ale

This was made specially for Yule. It consisted of hops, root ginger and treacle. This description comes from Aberdeen:

> *The earliest recollections I have of Christmas are associated with 'sids' being brought from the mealmill to be steepit for sowens, and with my being dispatched to Burnie's 'chop' for hops, ginger and a big flaggon of treacle, with which ingredients and malt from the Canal Heid [a public house], my mother brewed the Yule-ale.*
>
> Auld Lang Syne, W. Watson, 1903

Another type of ale was made from heather – ginger, hops and syrup was added. Honey was made into a drink called mead and Athole Brose was a creamy drink of honey, oatmeal and cream with the addition of two pints of whisky. It was stirred, if possible, with a silver spoon till it frothed then bottled and corked for several days.

Wine
This was made from the sap and berries of several trees, bushes and plants. Birch was popular, and rhubarb, elderberry, nettle and dandelion wines were prepared and laid down to mature.

Whisky
This was a Highland drink which did not, at least in any palatable form, reach the Lowlands until after the Jacobite Rebellion. It was, at first, classed as white wine.

> *Rum punch was, in fact, the universal beverage . . . and rum toddy was also . . . the never failing accompaniment of every supper. Whisky, in those days, being chiefly drawn from the large flat-bottomed stills of Kilbagie, Kennetpans and Loghrin, was only fitted for the most vulgar and fire-loving palates; but when a little of the real mountain-dew, from Glenlivet or Arran, could be obtained, which was a matter of difficulty and danger, it was sure to be presented to guests with as sparing a hand as the finest Maraschino di Zara.*
>
> *Glasgow and Its Clubs*, John Strang, 1864

Christmas lads
In the Highlands a group of men, in later years only boys, on Christmas Eve toured the houses dressed in white gowns and tall white hats. They lifted up the youngest child of the house and if there was none they made a baby out of a sheet or blanket and cradled it. This was 'Crist, Cristean – The Little Christ'. This infant, real or imagined was placed on a male lamb skin and carried three times around the fire deasil by the leader of the band. They sang the Christmas Hail.

> *Hail to the King, Hail to the King,*
> *Healthy round the hearth be ye.*
> Traditional

They made offerings to the Little Christ

Hey the gift, ho the gift,
Hey the gift on the living.
Traditional

Gifts were left and in return the lads were given bread, butter and crowdie, which they took away for a feast.

Song-men
There were several traditional carols and the carollers toured around the houses singing them. The leading singer was the song-man, his companions were the chorus-men. They were rewarded with two or three bannocks which were handed out of the house window. The song-man got half of every bannock while the remainder was divided between the chorus-men.

Yule shard
The now more common rite of ensuring that every part of the house was cleaned before midnight on Hogmanay was originally also practised on Christmas Eve. Nothing must be borrowed or lent and all work should be finished before midnight. If a piece of work was left unfinished by Christmas Day the woman who was knitting or making it was known as a yule-shard.

Yule-yaud
A new item to wear was essential at Christmas or the person was called a Yule-yaud.

Midnight services
Pre-Reformation these services were held throughout Scotland but disappeared after the adoption of Presbyterianism in the sixteenth century. After the Second World War they began to be held, especially in the 1950s in more and more Church of Scotland churches, and became acceptable. In recent years they have been full to capacity and on occasion there has been trouble because of young hooligans who have had too much to drink. In some city churches 'bouncers' have been on duty at the doors.

Animals
The bees were thought to leave their hives at three o'clock on Christmas morning swarm round and return. In many areas

especially in the Highlands the people believed that the cattle knelt in the byre on Christmas Eve. Some farmers went into the byre and stable on Christmas Eve and read a chapter of the Bible behind their cattle and horses to prevent them from harm.

Evergreens

As at all festivals greenery was brought into the house on Christmas Eve. At Christmas this was naturally evergreen branches. These plants symbolized the hope of undying life and their branches were thought to be magical because they ensured the return of vegetation and because they bore fruit in winter. From the time of the Druids mistletoe was considered sacred but after the introduction of Christianity it was frowned on by the chuch as pagan and was not included in church decorations. Holly and ivy were favourites. These were popular with the Romans who decked their homes with holly boughs at Saturnalia. In Rome the Christians did likewise so as not to draw attention to themselves and this custom came with them to Britain where it was adopted. Fir branches from the Scots pine or whin were originally used as torches to give light but became included in the decorations.

Holly

Boys used holly for divination. They deliberately pricked their thumb with the sharp edges of the leaves and counted the drops of blood as they fell. Each drop was supposed to equal a year of their lives and they could forecast when they would die. Prickly holly was considered male and smooth holly or she-holly, female, it was thought to give protection from lightning. Holly became an acceptable Christian symbol as its berries and prickly leaves were a reminder of the crown of thorns and the shedding of Jesus' blood during the Crucifixtion. Holly was never burned as it was thought that this brought death or misfortune to a family. It was always allowed to wither away.

Ivy

This was a fertility symbol. It was also grown on houses to frighten away witches. If it withered while growing on a house, there would be no direct heir in the family.

Yule-candle

The Yule-candle when lit was allowed to burn out naturally. It was then locked away in a chest to be brought out and relit on the occasion of the death of the head of the household during his lyke wake.

Christmas shopping

It was in the latter half of the nineteenth century when Christmas shopping in towns became popular. Brightly lit window displays encouraged browsing and shops often remained open till midnight on Christmas Eve.

> *Ye wha on ferlies like to gaze,*
> *Come busk ye wi' your brawest claes;*
> *Ye leddies don a dainty goon,*
> *Syne danner oot to view the toon.*
> *Here's Christmas cairds, a gran' array,*
> *The sweet an' braw, the rich an' gay,*
> *Wi' gloves an' muffs, an' scarves and ties,*
> *That bonniest lass an' lad must prize.*
> *There's fal-de-rals an' gew-gaws here,*
> *To suit the daft days o' the year;*
> *Rare pictur' books for youth or wean,*
> *An' toys micht fill a railway train.*

Melodies and Memories, John Black, 1909

Christmas Day

Letting Yule in

The first person to open the door of the house on Yule morning would prosper best that year. A table or chair was then placed in the doorway and covered with a clean cloth. Bread or bannocks and cheese were laid out and a new broom besom was placed beside the outer back door. This food was then offered to visitors.

Gifts

The giving of gifts to the poor was a part of the Roman Saturnalia and was also carried out during the Kalends – a period of three days when gifts were given in Rome in honour of Strenna, a goddess. Over the years gifts began to be given to children then to other members of the family and later also to friends. The Magi, who were a tribe of professional magicians from Persia, included amongst their members the Three Wise Men who brought gifts to the baby Jesus at Bethlehem. The Christian Church used this as a way of christianizing the giving of gifts at Yule.

Peter's payment
In Uist on the morning of Christmas Day the old men ask the young men to row 707 strokes from the shore before casting their lines. Any fish which are caught are given to the poor or elderly as a tribute to St Peter, king of fishermen.

Yule-bawbee
This was a penny or halfpenny given to each child in the family on Christmas Day. Oranges and nuts were other popular gifts. Women wrapped in shawls stood outside the doors of the theatres at Christmas selling from their baskets Seville oranges, at three for a penny.

First footing
This took place on Christmas Day as on many other festive occasions. The first foot must not come empty-handed but must carry bread, money and a peat to symbolize plenty food, wealth and warmth for the family during the season of Yule.

Father Christmas
In Norse mythology Odin, the gift-bringer, swept across the sky at midnight in his chariot which was drawn by his horse, Sleipnir. He gave gifts to those who were worthy of a reward and punished those who were wicked. Frey, also in Norse mythology, had a chariot drawn by boars, and the goddess Freya had a chariot drawn by two large black cats. She made the wives of the Vinili wrap their hair around their faces like beards to trick Odin into granting them victory over the Vandals.

In Russia merchants wore fur-trimmed garments to keep wrapped up from the cold. To cross the frozen wastes they rode on sleighs. Santa Claus was a mysterious supernatural being with dwarfs or 'Dueregar' who worked underground and helped him to make all the toys and gifts. All these myths became fused and produced an image of Santa Claus as a rotund man wearing a red fur-trimmed suit and long leather boots who travelled across the sky in a sleigh drawn by reindeer of which there were several herds in the Highlands of Scotland. He entered by the chimney because he could not pass the rowan twigs or holly which guarded the door.

Santa Claus

He was often known as Father Christmas but the name Santa Claus came from St Nicholas, Bishop of Myra in Calabria, Italy who was renowned as a giver of gifts to the poor and for doing good deeds without fuss. He travelled in Russia, Germany and Holland and his fame spread. There he was known as Sant Klaus. His feast day was on December the sixth and was banned, like all the other saints days, after the Reformation. His reappearance in the nineteenth century was due to Prince Albert, the Consort of Queen Victoria, who came from Germany.

Christmas tree

It was Prince Albert who also introduced the Christmas tree which was more popular in England than in Scotland until the middle of the twentieth century. The hanging on it of tinsel is akin to the cloth remnants which are left attached to a clootie well and are there to bring good luck. An older Druid tradition saw trees hung with pieces from the clothes of the victims who were sacrificed and bits of animal skin. The Romans during the Saturnalia decorated trees with lights.

Animals breakfast

It was the custom to give a special breakfast to the animals on Christmas Day morning. They got a sheaf of corn, and a sheaf of oats was hung on a rowan tree for the wild birds. Owners of cattle fed the beasts from their own hand on Yule morning.

Food and drink

A special effort was made by even the poorest to have a change of diet at Christmas. Those who had plenty shared it with the less fortunate and extra spice was added to dishes to make them more appetising.

But hirstle yont, see what a sicht,
O' holly leaves an' berries bricht,
An' bourocks big o' cake an' bun
To grace the feasts an' spice the fun.
Here's turkeys, geese, an' prime roast beef,
O' aulden Yule-tide fare the chief –
With or without may ilka yin,
Hae happiness the heart within

Melodies and Memories, John Black, 1909

Yule-tide loaves

These were loaves baked for Yule which were made of leavened rye. Other loaves known as mane bread were baked with an impression of Jesus or the Virgin Mary. Oat bread with rich seasoning was also prepared. This was very popular and eventually became a speciality of town bakers. In 1583 the baking of Yule bread was banned and the bakers or baxters were obliged to report the names of customers asking for Yule bread.

> *Five persons were adjudged to make public repentance because they kept the superstitious days of Yule, or Christmas, and the baxters were ordered to be inquired at when they baked Yule bread.*

Glasgow and Its Clubs, John Strang, 1864

Yule-sowens

Sowens were prepared on Christmas Eve but were not eaten until the small hours of Christmas Day. People invited their friends to join them for a feast of yule sowens. For luck some had to be left at the bottom of the dish. Sometimes trinkets were put into the mixture to add some fun to the proceedings. In the houses of the rich this was known as plum-porridge and included fruit. Flour was later added to this recipe and this was the origin of plum-pudding. Sowens were also added to the dough for scones and these were baked as a special treat at Yule-tide. A thinner version of yule-sowens was made, to which cream and honey was added, and this became a drink rather like Athole Brose. A spot of whisky gave the drink a kick.

Yule-kebbock

A cheese was specially made to be eaten at Yule. It had the additional ingredient of caraway seeds. Before they went out guising children would eat a piece of this cheese on an oatcake. If a slice should have a hole in it, this was thought to bring luck.

Yule-bannocks and brunies
They also received bannocks or oatcakes known as 'cake', made from a more refined meal than bannocks. Sometimes sugar or sowens were added. It was traditional to put trinkets for divination into the Yule bannock. It often had the edges furrowed to depict the rays of the sun and later was scored with the sign of the cross. In Shetland it was Yule-brunies made of fat and rye meal which had the traditional fluted edge. One was made for everyone who lived in the house.

Yule-meat
On Christmas Eve a sheep – a ewe – was killed for every household and called the yule-sheep. An ox was slaughtered and salted at Martinmas as a yule-mairt and it was eaten at Yule. It was often roasted on a spit over the Yule-log and a brose or thick soup was made with the stock. Yule-brose or fat brose was made in a large punchbowl, the mistress of ceremonies placing her wedding ring in it. The unmarried members of the company used their horn spoons to find the ring in the hope that it would bring them a spouse. From cottar to laird everyone ate fat brose on Christmas morning.

Goose
This was a favourite dish served on Christmas Day. Its remains would be turned into a goose pie or collops. Turkey first appeared in the reign of James VI and was a popular addition to the feast. The pagan reverence for the pig, who lived off the acorns of the sacred oak trees of the Druids, made the eating of its meat a taboo. The boar's head, favoured by the English, rarely featured on Scottish tables. Rabbits, hares and other meats such as lark's tongues, a delicacy, were eaten and game pies were popular amongst the gentry.

Mincemeat
Originally minced beef was an ingredient of mincemeat. Later only the fruit and spices remained but the pies were still traditionally called mince-pies. Those who now call them Christmas pies are probably more correct.

Yule-fish

Those who lived near the sea or who could afford to buy from the fishwife would buy fish and smoke it or have it smoked to eat during Yule. Smoked haddock was a great delicacy of the Christmas season.

How to spend Christmas

The way to respect Christmas time
Is not by drinking whisky or wine,
But to sing praises to God on Christmas morn,
The time that Jesus Christ, His Son was born;
Christmas time ought to be held most dear,
Much more so than the New Year,
Because that's the time that Christ was born,
Therefore respect Christmas morn.

Poetic Gems, William McGonagall, 1890

Sweetie Scone Day

Sweetie Scone Day was the name given to December the twenty-sixth. The sweetie scones, as opposed to sour scones, had the addition of fruit and spices. Boxing Day is a fairly recent addition in Scotland as, apart from the fees given on Christmas Eve, it was Handsell Monday, January the second, when tips were given in Scotland.

NEW YEAR

The Celtic New Year was celebrated at Samhain, November the first. Up until 1600 the Gregorian calendar placed New Year on March the twenty-fifth. This was still the beginning of the Scottish Legal Year up until 1752.

Passed this day at Holyrood an act of Privy Council, in which it is set forth that 'in all other weel-governit commonwealths and countries, the year begins yearly upon the first of January, commonly called New-year's Day, and that this realm only is different,' for which reason they ordained . . . that the next first of January shall be the first day of the year of God 1600.

Domestic Annals of Scotland, Vol 1, From the Revolution to the Rebellion 1745,
Robert.Chambers, 1874

These date changes account for the duplication of customs at both Christmas and New Year and, after the Reformation, the emphasis in Scotland, especially in the Lowlands, was entirely on New Year. With the movement of people during the Industrial and Agricultural Revolutions and the Highland Clearances of the nineteenth century customs in the Lowlands became intermingled with those of the Highlands and a strange mixture has survived.

Beggars warning
This notice was attached to the door of every church and religious house in Scotland on New Year's Day 1559.

> The blind, crooked, bedrels [bedfast], widows, orphans and all other poor, so visited by the hand of God as they may not work to the flocks of all Friars within the realm restitution for past wrongs, reformation for time to come.
>
> The Social Life of Scotland in the 18th Century, H.G. Graham, 1899

Blessing

> To those who bravely till the ground,
> And those who make the wheels go round,
> To those who dig the coal and shale,
> Those who succeed and those who fail,
> To weak or strong this word of cheer –
> We wish you all a Good New Year.
>
> Melodies and Memories, John Black, 1909

Tricks
Carrie-anker
At Burghead, on the thirtieth of December, it was traditional for boys to place dried seaweed in the oven to make it hard. They then hollowed it out and filled it with hemp which they set on fire and blew this through the key-holes of their neighbours' doors.

Dead cats
In Kintyre boys placed dead cats down the chimneys of anyone who had annoyed them during the closing year.

Door rapping and apple dooking

There's bairns wi' guizards at their tail
Cloutin' the door wi' runts o' kail
And fine ye'll hear the skruchs and skirls
O' lassies wi' their droukit curls
Bobbin' for apples i' the pail.

Songs of Angus, Violet Jacob, 1914

HOGMANAY

New Year's Eve was traditionally called Hogmanay. There is much controversy about its meaning. 'Hoggunott' was Norse for the 'Night of the slaughter' and referred to the killing of the beasts for the forthcoming festival. The toast was called 'the minnie – it was the Feast of Thor, hence, Hog-minnie, Thor-lor-lae. This was celebrated on December the twenty-fifth. It was transferred after the Reformation to December the thirty-first, the night before the New Year.

Rise up, gudewife, and shake your feathers,
Dinna think that we are beggars,
We're girls and boys come out to day,
For to get our Hogmanay,
Hogmanay, trol-lol-day.
Give us of your white bread and not of your gray,
Or else we'll knock your door all day.

Traditional

This was a rhyme tradtionally sung by children in the West of Scotland and was recorded as referring to Christmas Eve but gradually was transferred to Cake Night or Hogmanay. They held out their aprons and were rewarded with gifts of food. This change of date explains why similar customs were recorded on both occasions.

'Hug-me-nay ' or 'hawse and ney' were also suggested, meaning kiss me now, this being a popular custom. On the stroke of twelve even strangers kiss each other to celebrate the New Year. Even ladies in Sedan chairs were not immune from this habit. French influence occurs in 'Hoguinane' sung by children in France on the Scottish equivalent of Cake Day.

Cake Day

An ancient custom which is still observed by the children of
St Andrews is the collection of their 'cakes' from local shops
and houses on Hogmanay. As early as six o'clock on Tuesday
morning little groups of children set out, armed with baskets
and large paper bags, on a tour of the town, and were rewarded
with gifts of buns, shortbread, biscuits, chocolate, fruit, etc.
In some instances they were called upon to recite or sing before
receiving their cakes and the familiar lines which are most often
quoted were:

> *Ma feet's cauld*
> *Ma shoon's thin;*
> *Gie's ma cakes,*
> *An' let me rin.*

St Andrews Citizen, 4 January 1936

Cake Night

Folk went from house to house in the evening and ate cake and
cheese washed down with ale and whisky. Singing and dancing
were popular entertainment on such occasions.

> *The Auld Year's Night happened to be a Saturday and after*
> *all the houses had had their turn of 'caking' the wind up was*
> *in Wat's place.*

Kelso Chronicle, 30 December 1921

It is also recorded that Anstruther bakers made special cakes on
this day and petticoat biscuits with icing on top were popular.

Rituals
Ceremony of the hides

This was a custom observed in the Western Isles. The men
surrounded each house in turn carrying clubs and wearing
cow-hides complete with horns and hooves. Sometimes they
climbed onto the roof. They thrashed the walls with the clubs,
crying and shouting ancient rhymes. A rhyme accompanied
the beating.

> *Hogmanay of the sack,*
> *Hogmanay of the sack,*

Strike the hide,
Strike the hide.
Traditional

After this was chanted they would enter the house and sing:

Great good luck to the house
Good luck to the family,

Good luck to every rafter of it,
And to every wordly thing in it.
Good luck to horses and cattle,
Good luck to the sheep,
Good luck to every thing,
And good luck to all your means.
Luck to the good-wife,
Good luck to the children,
Good luck to every friend,
Great fortune and health to all.
Traditional

This gave protection to the house against fairies, demons or other spirits. A corner of the hide was singed in the fire and each person in the house had to smell this as a charm against injuries. Then they offered a stick which was wrapped in the breast-skin of a sheep, a deer or a goat. The man of the house singed this in the fire and carried it in his right hand three times deasil around each member of his family. Everyone was then given food and drink and after finishing their dram the party moved on to the next house.

Lucky coin
A silver-threepenny or sixpence was placed on the doorstep. If it was still there in the morning it would be a lucky year. Any new garment which had a pocket should have a silver coin carried in it on New Year's Day.

Yeel-gird
This was the name given to anyone who cried on New Year's Day as it was considered unlucky to shed tears on this day.

Communal celebrations

The tron, or weigh-building in many towns, had a clock tower. This or the market cross was the favourite gathering place of the townspeople around eleven o'clock on Hogmanay. As the witching hour of midnight approached the atmosphere was charged with excitement, as in many places it still is, as everyone waits for the bells to ring out the old year and ring in the new. Bagpipes were played and there was singing and dancing, hugging and kissing and shaking of hands while everyone wished everyone else 'A guid New Year'.

A guid New Year tae ane an' a',
An' mony may ye see;
An' during a' the years tae come,
O, happy may ye be.
An' may ye ne'er hae cause tae mourn,
Tae cry or shed a tear;
Tae ane an' a', baith great an' sma',
A hearty guid New Year.

A Guid New Year, P. Livingstone, 1848

Redding the house

This ritual cleaning, which also took place at Christmas in some areas, was done so that in the New Year a fresh beginning could be made. Floors were scrubbed, dishes scoured, the rok was emptied of yarn, which must then be made up into hanks, even the children were washed then, at a certain time well before midnight, all work stopped.

The following was the practice in my father's house in Partick,
about fifty to sixty years ago. On Hogmanay evening, children
were all washed before going to bed. An oat bannock was baked
for each child; it was nipped round the edge, had a hole in the
centre, and was flavoured with caraway seed. Great care was
taken that none of these bannocks should break in the firing as
such an occurrence was regarded as a very unlucky omen for
the child whose bannock was thus damaged. It denotes illness or
death during the year. Parents sat up till about half-past eleven,
when the fire was covered and every particle of ash swept up

and carried out of the house. All retired to bed before twelve o'clock, as it was unlucky not to be in bed as the New Year came in.

Folklore and Superstitious Beliefs in the West of Scotland within this Century,
James Napier, 1879

This is the exact opposite of most reports of Hogmanay customs when the celebrations usually begin at midnight and continue till the wee sma' hours.

Juniper
In Dingwall and Easter Ross this was cut after sunset on Hogmanay and was brought down to the farms where it was burned in front of cattle to purify them and guard them from evil. In other areas the juniper was dried out by the fire and later carried burning through the house.

Unspoken water
'Unspoken water' was water, taken from a stream or river over which the living and the dead passed, and collected without a word being spoken. Every member of the household must take a drink of it then the remainder was sprinkled over the beds for luck and protection.

First footing
First footing had its own rituals. Some people were, and some still are, superstitious about not being in their own house on the stroke of twelve. They fear that bad luck, illness or death will overtake the family. The first person to cross their threshold would also indicate the sort of year which lay ahead. The person should preferably be male, dark-haired and should carry a piece of peat or coal, a sum of money and a piece of cake and his bottle. These symbolized warmth, wealth, health and prosperity.

Ships' sirens
On the stroke of twelve all ships in port sounded their horns.

NEW YEAR'S DAY

Food and drink

Whisky

This was the traditional drink associated with New Year in the Highlands and became popular in the Lowlands after the Jacobite Rebellions. It gave offence if a drink was refused and preferably the glass should always be drained, at one swallow if possible.

Luck

A glass of whisky was poured by the head of the house immediately after 'the bells'. The glass was handed to his wife who took the first sip then passed it to every female present. The man of the house then topped it up for every sip drunk, he took a sip then passed it deasil around the men to bring luck to the family.

Het pint

This was made from spiced ale to which sugar, eggs, and spirits were added. Nutmeg was a favourite addition. Kettles of this beverage were carried around on Hogmanay as well as bottles of whisky and other drinks.

Sowens

In Aberdeen in the sixteenth and seventeenth centuries a cog of sowens, with the addition of honey and whisky, was carried round by first footers.

Short-bread

Made with creamed butter and sugar with the addition of fine flour this was often made in patterned wooden trays. A thistle was popular and the edge was always crimped to symbolize the rays of the sun.

Black bun

This is a heavy fruit cake made of nuts and spices in a pastry casing.

Steak pie

This was always a favourite dish at New Year. The steak was thickened with kidney gravy and was covered with flaky pastry and baked in a large ashet with a china funnel in its centre to prevent the pastry from going soggy. Many butchers still have to work long hours in the week leading up to New Year.

Games
Shinty matches
In Kintyre a game of shinty was played on New Year's Day. This often ended in injury to one or more players and fighting broke out on most occasions because the players were the worse for drink – in 1836 a man was killed.

Football
Games of football were often played on New Year's Day in the streets and in the twentieth century it was traditional to hold local derbys with professional teams drawing big crowds for the Ne'erday game.

Yule-pins
Te-totum was a game played by children at Yuletime. When it was played, the stake was a pin.

Handsel Monday
Gifts were given on the Old New Year, January the twelfth, and in some areas it was celebrated as a holiday up until the beginning of the twentieth century. In other places it was the first Monday after New Year, Old style. Handsel Monday was like the English Boxing Day when employers gave bonuses or gifts to their employees. It began after midnight and was a repeat of New Year with more visiting when songs and ballads, often derisory and with local names substituted, were sung or recited. Young men walked in procession with torches and blew horns. Scotch broth, haggis and black and white puddings were eaten and in the morning the fair may have been set up and the fun continued. There were usually dances held in the evening. The next day it was back to auld claes an' porridge.

Uphalieday
This was the name for Twelfth Night in Scotland. It is the night when all traces of decorations must be removed. A type of Dundee cake was popular on Twelfth Night and parties were

held where all the fripperies of balloons, paper trumpets, paper hats and confetti were seen.

Lucky fardin

A piece of dough used to bake the New Year cake was kept until Twelfth Night and a farthing, a quarter of a penny, was placed in it. When the scones were baked, the person finding the 'lucky fardin' would have good luck during the year.

Forfeits

The 'Twelve Days of Yule' was a game of forfeits played in a semi-circle. A rhyme was spoken by each person in turn and if they made a mistake a forfeit was paid.

The king sent his lady on the first Yule day,
A papingo-aye;
Wha learns my carol and carries it away.

The king sent his lady on the second Yule day,
Three partriks, a papingo-aye;
Wha learns my carol and carries it away.

The king sent his lady on the third Yule day,
Three plovers, three partriks, a papingo-aye;
Wha learns my carol and carries it away.

The king sent his lady on the fourth Yule day,
A goose that was gray,
Three plovers, three partriks, a papingo-aye;
Wha learns my carol and carries it away.

The king sent his lady on the fifth Yule day,
Three starlings, a goose that was gray,
Three plovers, three partriks, a papingo-aye;
Wha learns my carol and carries it away.

The king sent his lady on the sixth Yule day,
Three goldspinks, three starlings, a goose that was gray,
Three plovers, three partriks, a papingo-aye;
Wha learns my carol and carries it away.

The king sent his lady on the seventh Yule day,
A bull that was brown, three goldspinks,

Three starlings, a goose that was gray,
Three plovers, three partriks, a papingo-aye;
Wha learns my carol and carries it away.

The king sent his lady on the eighth Yule day,
Three ducks a merry laying, a bull that was brown,
Three goldspinks, three starlings, a goose that was gray,
Three plovers, three partriks, a papingo-aye;
Wha learns my carol and carries it away.

The king sent his lady on the ninth Yule day,
Three swans a merry swimming,
Three ducks a merry laying, a bull that was brown,
Three goldspinks, three starlings,
A goose that was gray,
Three plovers, three partriks, a papingo-aye;
Wha learns my carol and carries it away.

The king sent his lady on the tenth Yule day,
An Arabian baboon, three swans a merry swimming,
Three ducks a merry laying, a bull that was brown,
Three goldspinks, three starlings,
A goose that was gray,
Three plovers, three partriks, a papingo-aye;
Wha learns my carol and carries it away.

The king sent his lady on the eleventh Yule day,
Three hinds a merry hunting, an Arabian baboon,
Three swans a merry swimming,
Three ducks a merry laying, a bull that was brown,
Three goldspinks, three starlings, a goose that was gray,
Three plovers, three partriks, a papingo-aye;
Wha learns my carol and carries it away.

The king sent his lady on the twelfth Yule day,
Three maids a merry dancing, three hinds a merry hunting,
An Arabian baboon, three swans a merry swimming,
Three ducks a merry laying, a bull that was brown,
Three goldspinks, three starlings, a goose that was gray,
Three plovers, three partriks, a papingo-aye;
Wha learns my carol and carries it away.

The king sent his lady on the thirteenth Yule day,
Three stalks o' merry corn, three maids a merry dancing,
An Arabian baboon, three swans a merry swimming,
Three ducks a merry laying, a bull that was brown,
Three goldspinks, three starlings, a goose that was gray,
Three plovers, three partriks, a papingo-aye;
Wha learns my carol and carries it away.

Traditional

Snapdragon

A dish of raisins had brandy poured over it and set alight. Each person tried to snatch a raisin without burning their fingers. If they succeeded they could make a wish but must not tell anyone what it was or it could not come true.

Fire Festivals
and False Faces

FIRE FESTIVALS

*F*ire was a symbol of the sun and from the beginning of time; it was worshipped for its life-giving rather than its life-destroying properties. Fire was extremely important and was considered a purifying agent. It gave heat for cooking, warmth, comfort and light. It destroyed germs and disease. It drove away wild animals and kept evil spirits at bay. Because of these properties bonfires were central to many festivals. Brands and torches, which were small fires were used in ceremonies and at midnight on Beltane, Hallowe'en and Yule – the moments when the other-world was at its most dangerous – fire became an essential part in guarding against and defeating the powers of evil. Sacrifices were burned, cattle passed over or through it and people leapt across it in the belief that they would be protected from ill-luck.

BURNING OUT THE OLD YEAR

The custom of burning out the old year was an expurgation of ills which had beset the populace the previous year and offered hope for fertility and a good harvest in the coming year.

Bonfires
Biggar

A very old ceremony of lighting a yule fire took place in Biggar at the place where the old market cross once stood. It was lit before the bells and there were fireworks hidden in it which exploded. Red herrings were toasted in the fire and eaten. At the 'chappin' o' the twal' silence reigned and then a great cheer and singing of 'Auld Lang Syne' broke out to greet the New Year.

> *Should auld aquaintance be forgot,*
> *And never brocht to min' ?*
> *Should auld aquaintance be forgot,*
> *And auld lang syne.*
>
> *For auld lang syne, my dear,*
> *For auld lang syne,*
> *We'll tak a cup o' kindness yet*
> *For auld lang syne. . .*
>
> *And there's a haun my trusty fiere,*
> *An' gies a haun o' thine,*
> *And we'll tak a right gude-willie-waught,*
> *For auld lang syne.*

Auld Lang Syne, Robert Burns, 1793

Wick

Material for the bonfire began to be collected in November and it was carried up Shilling Hill to be built into a massive bonfire. Later this was transferred to the Bignold Park where everyone gathered on Hogmanay to celebrate the New Year.

Idolatry

Complaints were made in the seventeenth and eighteenth centuries about idolatrous and superstitious practices of carrying lit torches around the boundaries of houses and farms. In 1655 ministers in Moray complained of the torches being circled around boats in the harbours on Hogmanay.

Flambeaux

At Comrie on Hogmanay there was a procession of torch bearers dressed in fantastic costumes, some with horned headdresses.

On the stroke of twelve the bagpipes start up, torches are lit and paraded round the town.

Stonehaven

At Stonehaven balls of material soaked in tar were lit and paraded up and down the town as soon as the bells rang. They were swung round their heads to frighten away the witches.

Children

Children would light a stick and turn around swinging it in a circle around themselves so that no evil spirits or fairies would harm them.

Tar-barrels
Campbeltown

On Hogmanay in Campbeltown as soon as the town clock struck twelve a procession arrived at the Cross in the Longrow. Five men were chosen to carry the blazing tar barrels and they raced to be first at the gathering point. Spectators roared them on. An old boat was filled with the burning barrels and dragged on its keel to the site of a bonfire where it burned gaily amidst great celebration. This custom ended in 1881 and some folk in the town were delighted.

> *No more will we be subjected to the horrors of violent nocturnal bell-ringing, the coarse 'Hooray! boys, Hooray!', the horrible smell of burning tar, the lurid glare that made one think of the regions descended by Dante, the oaths and ribaldry, and the persistent attempts to extort backsheeth [beg] – all have vanished.*
>
> *Campbeltown Courier*, January 1881

Galloway

The carrying of tar barrels also took place in Minigaff and Newton Stewart up until the First World War. The young men formed a Tar Barrel Association and collected barrels, not always legitimately, in readiness for Hogmanay. Three villages joined in the torchlight procession, Minigaff, Blackcraig and Newton Stewart. The participants were in fancy-dress and rode on horseback across the River Cree. At midnight burning tar barrels were carried through each place and set on the bonfires.

Lerwick

In the nineteenth century on January the thirtieth, a large sledge filled with tar barrels was hauled from the docks into the town by the menfolk, usually in disguise, to the accompaniment of blaring horns. At an appointed place a fight broke out between those from the north and south ends of the town. This ceased at 4.00 a.m when a gun was fired. This festival was discontinued in 1874 owing to rowdiness.

Burning the Clavie

The Clavie was the name given to a basket in which fire was carried around the fishing boats for protection and good luck. The ceremony was popular up until the sixteenth century when it was banned in many places as idolatrous and leading to rowdiness.

Burghead

The Burning of the Clavie survives at Burghead, in Moray, an area where many traces of the Picts have been found. A dispute broke out over whether it should be held on the old new year or transferred to the new. The 'new stylers' were defeated and it is still held on January the eleventh, old Hogmanay. A team of five chosen men who must be locals appoint a Clavie King. They prepare the Clavie using old tools which must be borrowed. It would be unlucky for any money to change hands. A tar barrel is broken in two. The lower half is fixed to the Spoke, the name given to the salmon-fishing stake which is about eight feet in length, by a single nail which a blacksmith has forged for this purpose. No metal must touch it and it is hammered in with a smooth stone. The remainder of the barrel is then broken and attached two inches apart around the bottom of the Clavie and the spoke, leaving room for a man's head. It is filled with tar-soaked wood and shavings with a space in the centre for the blazing peat.

At six o'clock the youngest member is sent to the house of a lucky person for a live peat. To a cry of 'There go the witches' the Clavie is set alight. The Clavie bearer ducks his head under the Spoke and lifts the Clavie onto his shoulders. His is an important role as the good luck of the community hangs on his shoulders. He must not stumble or ill-luck will follow. The procession sets out around the harbour and the old town. Pieces of the Clavie are thrown into open doorways for luck and eventually it reaches its home at the Doorie Hill, the place where the Druids lit their fires. A pillar was built to house it in 1809. It has tar added and the blaze can be seen across the Moray Firth. The King then climbs up onto the pillar and begins to destroy the Clavie. Everyone scrambles to obtain a piece to take home for luck and to fend off witches.

Hail! Worthy Chief of Clavie fame
Lang may you live to burn the same
And fleg the witches frae oor hame
Far ower the sea.
We think it richt and fair to name your Jubilee.

For fifty years ye've seen her burned
Yet never did ye see her turned
But often have ye seen her spurned
By some new stylers;
Tho' aye the coal tar weel she churned
Amangst revilers.

They tried fu' hard tae change the nicht
But losh! It was an awfu' sicht.
The natives ran wi' a' their micht
And broke the barrell;
New 'stylers' ran in such a plicht,
man, didn't they snarl.

They'll never try tae dae the same
As sure as Peterkin's your name
An' tho' it was an' awfu' sin,
Their sins were mony.
Tae change the nicht, and sic a din
But wasna' canny.

Some learned folk say its superstition,
If so, the Bible's no worth sneeshin,
For in't we have, as a petition
Tae burn a witch.
This law has come to full fruition
'Mang poor and rich.

This nicht ye've gien's another treat,
Which naething on the earth can beat,
And 'Katie Clavers' aye ye'll cheat
And break her charms.
As soon's she sees the lowin peat
Her temper warms.

With dusht ire and with fear,
She leaves us for anithir year,
Nor does she e'en tak time to speer
Aboot the cheering,
Across the Firth she's seen tae steer
For Norway veering.

Long may ye live tae draw the nail,
Live tae mak' witches and warlocks quail,
Live on, though you are getting frail
Years yet tae see.
Chief of the Clavie, hail, all hail,
Your Jubilee.

James Peterkin, *Chief of the Clavie on his Jubilee,*
R.G. Dick, 1890

Burning the Crate

This was carried out in several places but gradually died out as it was considered dangerous and banned. It was believed to date back to the time of the Picts when they burned effigies of Jarl Thorfinn, the Norse invader. In Dingwall it was a large crate which was filled in secret in the woods where the young men had hidden an old horse for several weeks and fed it well to make it ready for its task of drawing the crate through the town on Hogmanay.

Home-made instruments were also concocted for the band – whistles, drums, wire triangles and tambourines. These would make enough noise to drive away any evil spirits. A Red Indian, dressed in bright colours, rode the horse and other fantastic figures danced alongside. On reaching the High Street the crate was set alight and it was pulled up to the Mercat Cross. At midnight the contents of the crate were scattered and people tried to keep a piece for luck.

Burning the boat

A ceremony of burning the boat was held at Bettyhill and in some North-East fishing villages. For many years, at Cockenzie in East Lothian at the Fishermen's Walk in September, a boat was burned on the Boat Shore and fireworks were exploded.

Up-Helly-aa

This festival, held in Lerwick, originally was on the last day of Yule but was moved to the last Tuesday of January. Jarl Thorfinn, the scourge of the Picts, is again represented. Several squads of eight to ten young men prepare for many months for the festival. A full-size galley complete with shields and oars is voluntarily built and painted, and five-foot torches are prepared. In the early evening of the last Tuesday it is drawn to its starting place and by 7.30 p.m. it is on its way. Guizer Jarl steps on board – a flare is fired by the previous Jarl and immediately thirty more flares appear all along the ship. The large torches are lit from these flares and the procession moves off. The Viking warriors, dressed in splendid costumes, walk alongside followed by the squads which are balloted for position. They are dressed in a variety of themes. The traditional Up-Helly-aa song is sung as they move to the site of the burning. The Galley song follows and the galley is surrounded by torches. Guizer Jarl calls for three cheers for the builders and he is cheered as he descends from the ship. A bugle call signals the torching of the galley. Fun and festivity go on all night as Shetlanders celebrate their historic links with the Norsemen.

DISGUISE

Going in disguise was one of the oldest customs. It was adopted on many occasions and for different purposes. Even if someone watching knew who the person behind the disguise was, it was unlucky for them to name him or her. Masks, false-faces, animal heads and skins, costumes and grotesque features were used for disguise. There are few descriptions, except perhaps the Gyro, a giantess in Orkney, which would suggest that the enormous heads and caricatures found on the Continent of Europe at Mardi Gras were ever popular in Scotland.

Guising

Guising was carried out by adults as well as children and not only at Hallowe'en but on several occasions in the year. Many records and old documents show that this practice took place at Easter, May Day, Hallowe'en, Martinmas, Christmas and New Year. Adults, both men and women, went around the neighbourhood in disguise, with blackened faces – usually soot or burnt cork was used – and expected to be received with gifts of food and drink. In some areas invited guests would arrive on Hallowe'en, Hogmanay or Twelfth Night wearing fantastic costumes and always masked.

Cross-dressing

The Roman Saturnalia encouraged cross-dressing and masquerades. Slaves donned the dress of their masters and masqueraded as people of importance without fear of reprisals. This was not always apppreciated in Scotland with its more Calvinistic approach to life. Complaints were made by the General Assembly of the Church of Scotland and by local ministers, reporting about their parish in the *First Statistical Account of Scotland*, 1796, against men in women's clothing and women in men's, during festivals.

> *A sort of secret society of Gysarts made itself notorious in several of the neighbouring villages, men dressed as women and women men, dancing together in a most unseemly way.*
> The History of Lanark, A. Robertson, reprinted, 1974

> *Two lads disguised themselves, to be play at 'guisards' at New Year festivities; they blackened their faces – one dressed as a woman, the other put straw ropes round his legs, and for this innocent iniquity they were summoned before the Session. Both acknowledged their sin and promised by God's grace never to fall into the likes again.*
> Minutes of the Kirk Session of Clackmannan, July 1713

Blackening

The idea behind the blackening of faces goes back to the time of the Druids who rubbed themselves with the ashes of the sacrificial fires for luck.

Court guisers

On Uphallie Day or Twelfth Night guisers paid for by the Court took part in the festivities.

> *Item (the fifth day of Januar was Uphaly Day) in Edinburgh*
> *that nycht to the gyaris, at the King's command.*
> The Lord High Treasurer's Account, 1496

Court guisers appeared on many occasions in the year and performed whenever the Court was held. This included Arbroath, Linlithgow and Stirling. In other records it appears that the King and his retinue themselves indulged in guising and mummery.

Straw costumes

In Shetland men wore straw suits as disguise as they went from door to door at Hallowe'en, Martinmas and Christmas accompanied by a piper. They also covered their faces with coloured handkerchiefs. They were rewarded with a dram of whisky and money. In Sutherland they wore straw hats decorated with ribbons and in Perthshire a straw kilt, jacket and stockings cross-gartered, which meant laced with heather rope.

Widdershins

If anyone refused to admit the guisers or give them gifts they would circle the fire against the sun or widdershins. In some places they built a cairn of stones outside to let others know of their reception and together these were the equivalent of putting a curse on the house and its occupants. They also stamped loudly on the ground as if shaking the dust of it from their feet before intoning the malediction.

> *The malison of God and of Hogmanay be on you,*
> *And the scathe of the plaintive buzzard,*
> *Of the hen-harrier, of the raven, of the eagle,*
> *And the scathe of the sneaking fox.*
> *The scathe of the dog and of the cat be on you,*
> *Of the boar, of the badger and of the brugha,*
> *Of the hipped bear and of the wild wolf,*
> *And the scathe of the foul foumart.*
> Carmina Gadelica, Alexander Carmichael, 1899

A more modern version of the same idea was popular in Perth.

> *Tramp, tramp, tramp, the boys are marchin',*
> *We are the guisers at the door,*
> *If ye dinae let us in,*
> *We will bash yer windies in*
> *An' ye'll never see the guisers anymore.*
>
> Traditional

Candlemas

Guising also took place at Candlemas, which was not only a rural festival but was also celebrated in the larger towns, where the usual custom of going from door to door in disguise, reciting and singing, occurred. On St Thomas' Day, December the twenty-first, a dole (a share or gift) was requested and a sprig of holly given in return.

Hallowe'en

In Brechin, up until 1925, a carnival was held on Hallowe'en when folk took to the streets and a parade was held which included decorated floats.

Caking

Guising, because of the interference and fines of the Kirk, was gradually left to the children. They made the most of these occasions and in every part of Scotland regularly sought an excuse for dressing up, blackening their faces or donning masks to ask for their cakes.

> *Pieces of fancy-bread or currant loaf as customarily given to*
> *children requesting such on the morning of Old New Year's Day.*
> Dictionary of the Scottish Tongue, J. Grant, ed. 1929

> *My feet's cauld, my shoon's done,*
> *Gie's my cakes and let's run.*
> Traditional

They would then hold out their aprons which would already be filling up with bannocks or tea bread.

Pleas

A wide variety of verses are used when asking to be allowed in.

From the simple, 'Please give me my Hallowe'en?' to the polite request in Langholm, 'Are ye wantin' ony guisers?' There householders were allowed to guess who the guisers were. If they didn't find the right names they were told them before the children departed. In Kirkcaldy it was:

> *Please to help the guisers, please to open your door,*
> *Please for tae gie us an apple frae yer store?*
>
> Traditional

In Aberdeen when requested to perform by the householders a favourite was:

> *Hallowe'en ae nicht at e'en,*
> *Three witches tae be seen,*
> *Ane black an' twa green,*
> *An' a' cryin' Hallowe'en.*
>
> Traditional

Performances

When Sir Walter Scott was a boy, bands of youths would tour the countryside during Yule dressed specifically as Biblical characters. This, he thought, was a very old custom which perhaps originated in the religious 'mystery plays'.

King of Macedon

> *In my boyhood we were wont to take the characters of the*
> *apostles, at least of Peter, Paul and Judas Iscariot; the first*
> *had the keys, the second carried a sword and the last the bag*
> *in which the dole of our neighbours' plum cake was deposited.*
> *One played a champion and recited some traditional rhymes;*
> *another was Alexander, King of Macedon who conquered*
> *all the world but Scotland alone. There was also, occasionally*
> *a St George.*
>
> *The Poetical Works*, Walter Scott, 1897

This must have been a version of the well-known play *Galation* which dated back to the Pagan era. At one time it was performed in May but later this was transferred to Hallowe'en or Hogmanay.

There was a confused resemblance to the ancient mysteries,
in which the characters of Scripture, the Nine Worthies,
and other popular personages were usually exhibited.
The Poetical Works, Walter Scott, 1897

Galation

The boys went around the neighbourhood, knocking at various doors. The principal characters were the hero, Galation, the Black Knight, the Doctor, Judas, who was the purse bearer, and a lad who acted as a chorus. The hero was killed in a fight over a lady but was revived by the doctor.

In the Burgh of Peebles, in 1847, Galation was dressed in a white shirt, tied round the middle with a handkerchief, from which hung a wooden sword. He had a large cocked hat of white paper, either cut out with little human profiles or pasted over with penny valentines.

Here come I Galation.
Galation is my name,
Sword and buckler by my side,
I hope to win the game.
Traditional

The purse bearer offered his bag to the householder and received gifts of bannocks, fruit and nuts.

The White Boys of Yule

Boys move around the countryside during the Christmas
holidays dressed all in white. One of them is called Belzebub.
They act out a play and expect the householder to give them an
offering of food or money. It is a very old theme where two
knights argue over a lady. They fight, one is badly wounded
then in some areas Belzebub comes and cures him, in others it
is a doctor.

> *Here come I, auld Belzebub,*
> *And over my shoulder I carry a club;*
> *And in my hand a frying-pan,*
> *Sae don't ye think I'm a joly auld man?*
> *Christmas comes but once a year,*
> *And when it comes it brings good cheer.*

The knights enter and proceed to fight until one falls when he calls out

A doctor! a doctor, or I die –
A doctor! a doctor! here am I.
What can you cure?

Belzebub replies

All disorders to be sure,
The gravel and the gout,
The rotting of the snout;
If the devil be in you,
I can blow him out.
Cut off legs and arms,
Join them too again,
By the virtue of my club,
Up Jack, and fight a main.

Scottish Gallovidian Encyclopedia, John Mactaggart, 1824

Other reports of Yule Boys describe them as having their faces blackened with soot and wearing a sheepskin woolly-side-out belted around the middle with a straw rope.

Plays

Plays were a popular part of festivals and also a name sometimes given to festivals and fairs. Before the Reformation even the king took part in Robin Hood frolics. The fact that plays of any kind were banned after the Reformation does not seem to have caused the populace much of a problem. That they continued to enjoy certain pageants and plays is obvious from old records.

The Provost, Baillies, and Counsele ordaines the Thesaurer to pay the werkmen, merchandis, carteris, paynteris, and utheris that furnisht the graith [workhorse] to the convoy of the Moris to the Abbey, and of the plai [sic] maid thair at Saturday, the tent day Junii, the soume of £38.16.2d.

Municipal Records of Edinburgh, 15th January 1554

Play fields

The plays were a feature of burgh life. Edinburgh, Aberdeen, Glasgow, Dundee, Perth, Haddington and Stirling had permanent play fields used for sports and plays. In Edinburgh in 1578 complaint was made in Kirk Session Records about the behaviour of those who in May took part in

> *insolent plays, as King of May, Robin Hood and such others, in the month of May, played either by bairnies at the school or others. . .*

and the Lothian question was asked,

> *What ought to be done to sick persons that, after admonition, will passe to May playis, and especially elders and deacons, and others quha bear office in the Kirk?*

The answer given being,

> *They ought not to be admitted to the sacrament without satisfaction, in special elders and deacons.*

Another curious fact was that Play Sundays continued until 1599 when the Presbytery of Aberdeen ordered 'that there be nae play-Sundays hereafter, under all hiest pain', *Annals of the Presbytery of Aberdeen*, 1599.

Satire
Sir David Lindsay, wrote and had performed, in 1531, *Ane Satyr of the Thrie Estaits* which poked fun at Church and State. It played before the Court at Linlithgow in 1540 on Uphallie Day.

Montrose

> *The 4th* [of February], *several young gentlemen of this place acted Mr. Allan Ramsay's celebrated 'Pastoral Comedy' , for the diversion of the gentlemen and ladies about this town, with all dresses suitable, and performed it with so much spirit and humour, as agreeably surprised the whole audience; to oblige whom they re-enacted it and the farce of the 'Mock Doctor' two succeeding nights. The money taken. . . was distributed among the poor.*

> *Caledonian Mercury*, 9th February, 1735

Play-mare
This was a hobby horse which seems to have played a major part in many entertainments at Yule and on other occasions.

This was made from a wooden frame which fitted around a man's waist and was decorated with cloth, leather and bells.

Abbot of Unreason

The celebrations in many towns were supervised by a paid individual who was appointed in some places from Hallowe'en until Yule or Candlemas and in others all year round. He was comparable to the Lord of Misrule of the Saturnalia and hosted the most anarchic, libellous and blasphemous events which could take place without any repercussions.

Purpose

His job was to 'hold the town in gladness and blythness with dances, farces, plays, and games in times convenient.' He also presided over the Christmas gambols with dictatorial authority and he had to make the prologue and epilogue at plays. Sometimes he had to take to the stage during the intervals and also act as Master of Ceremonies.

> *Under the garb of a dignified clergyman, he entertained the licentious rabble with his absurdities.*
> *History of Edinburgh,* Hugo Arnot 1779

Names

In Aberdeeen he was known as the Abbot of Bonaccord or goodwill, in Edinburgh – Abbot of Narent (nae rent – a pun on his free lodgings) and Lord of Inobedience. In other places as the Abbot of Unreason or Out of Reason and in Peebles as The Lord of Unrest. He was a Prince of Revels or King of Saturnalia.

Funding

The burgh funds supplied these personages with money for fancy embroidered coats, minstrels and gunpowder for squibs and fireworks. There were occasionally complaints that he overspent. In 1553 the Abbot of Bonaccord got into trouble with the town council of Aberdeen for giving too many feasts in May and was limited to three banquets. He was told to put on general plays, dances and games as had been 'used and wont.'

Boy Bishop

The Boy Bishop was another appointee who took part in revels.

A Boy Bishop's procession took place in several towns on St Nicholas' Eve, December the sixth. Collections were uplifted. His term of office terminated on Innocents Day, December the twenty-sixth.

Idolatry

What would appear, under any other circumstances, to be called idolatry was tolerated. The mock abbot and his motley crew invaded churches and mimicked the rituals and services.

> *The mock dignatory was a stout-made under-sized fellow,*
> *whose thick squab form had been made grotesque by a*
> *supplemental paunch, well-stuffed. He wore a mitre of*
> *leather, with the front like a grenadier's cap, adorned with*
> *mock embroidery, and trinkets of tin . . . His robe was of*
> *buckram and his cope of canvas; curiously painted and cut*
> *into open work. On one shoulder was fixed the painted figure*
> *of an owl; and he bore in his right hand his pastoral staff . . .*
> *The attendants of this mock dignitary . . . followed their*
> *leader in regular procession into the church in his train,*
> *shouting as they came –*
> > *'A hail! A hail! for the venerable Father Howleglas,*
> > *the learned Monk of Misrule,*
> > *and the Right Reverend Abbot of Unreason.'*
>
> The Abbot, Walter Scott, 1820

They go on to cause mayhem by fumigating the church with burnt wool and feathers; they also put polluted water in the holy water basins and sang rude songs.

> *The bishop rich, he could not preach*
> *For sporting with the lasses;*
> *The silly friar behoved to fleech*
> *For awmous as he passes.*
> *The curate his creed*
> *He could not read –*
> *Sing haytrix, trim-go-trix*
> *Under the greenwood tree.*
>
> A parody on Godly and Spiritual Songs, Andro Hart, 1578

King of the Bean

A king of revels was appointed for Uphallie Day or Twelfth Night. He was called the King of the Bean. At the University of St Andrews it was called the Feast of Kings. The four ladies-in-waiting of Mary, Queen of Scots (Mary Fleming, Mary Beaton, Mary Seaton, and Mary Carmichael) were known as 'the Four Maries'. Mary Beaton was elected Queen of the Bean and likewise Mary Fleming, in 1563, held that position. She was dressed in silver and jewels. The function of these majesties was to act as Master or Mistress of Ceremony and keep the fun rolling with games, charades, forfeits and to supervise the removal of all the decorations.

Riding the Marches

BOUNDARIES

*T*erritorial boundaries were very important in the Middle Ages. Up until the twelfth century, in Scotland, the ownership of land tended to be by brute strength rather than by law. Land was owned by the Crown or by the Church. King David I began creating burghs with power to hold courts but it was his grandson, William the Lion who granted charters to many towns.

Charters
These charters declared certain towns to be burghs with rights to appoint a provost and baillies (magistrates) with power to hold courts and fairs and a duty to charge harbour dues, where appropriate, and to provide a tron and standards for weighing goods.

Burghs
Royal Burghs
Part of the agreement was that Royal Burghs would supply men for a fighting force in support of the king, and that they would set up a watch which would act 'wisely and busily'. They also paid rent and customs dues to the king. Under this charter

the right of the townspeople or burgesses to graze cattle on the common and to grow crops was made legal. In this way the land was held in direct partnership with the king. The charter also gave the right to hold an annual fair or fairs and weekly markets at a stated time. Another right was that 'fewel' (peat) 'faill' (turf) and 'divots' (thin turf used for thatching) could be cut from the common and carried away. These Royal Burghs were Aberdeen, Berwick, Crail, Dunfermline, Edinburgh, Elgin, Haddington, Inverkeithing, Linlithgow, Peebles, Perth, Roxburgh, Rutherglen and Stirling.

Burghs of Barony
These were also proclaimed by charter but the rights came to the burgesses indirectly. The charter was in favour of the landlord or superior who in turn made an agreement with the burgesses. The taxes were paid to him and he paid his dues to the king.

Burghs of Regality
These were burghs which had the Church as a superior – either an abbot or his secular representative.

Rivalry
There was rivalry between Perth and Dundee and an argument over who held the finest equestrian procession on the Riding of the Estates in 1567.

Inspection of the marches
Although this custom is usually associated with the Lowlands the boundaries were also inspected in parts of the Highlands.

> The Head Court orders that the land marches and privileges of the Burgh be furthwith visited and immediat visited and perambulat.
>
> Annals of Banff, W. Cramond, 1720

These inspections in the Borders are known as the Common Ridings. They are still held in the Borders with more fervour than in other parts of Scotland. The people of the Highlands, after 1745, were not encouraged to promote clan or civic loyalty.

Marches of Glasgow

In 1579 the procession at the Riding of the Marches on June the twentieth at Summerhill, Cowcaddens, included two minstrels dressed in blue coats with 'cramosie' (crimson velvet) embroidered with the arms of the city, a 'snap-maker' (gunmaker), 'ladleman' (a man who collected ladle duty), a 'tabroner' (drummer) and a fool.

> *In preparation for the Whitsunday Court and perambulation of the marches, the town council, on 2nd June 1599 ordained that every person absent from the play and pastime, which was appointed to take place on the following Thursday, and which had been duly proclaimed, should be subjected to a fine of £5 (Scots).*
>
> Early Glasgow, Vol 3, J.D. Marwick, 1915

Eight officers and two minstrels were to accompany them and a sum of money was made available for cloaks of red linsey-woolsey cloth.

March Stones

The boundaries of a burgh were marked with march stones. These were usually actual stones but could be part of a wall, set in a ditch or in the middle of a river or burn. It was a legal duty of the dignitaries to arrange for these to be inspected annually to ensure that no-one had interfered with them.

> *The haill burgesses and inhabitants, horse and foot, to attend Magistrates and Council, in their best equipage, to ride the commonities.*
>
> Charter of the Burgh of Peebles, 1134

Annual inspections were carried out, usually on horseback, when every inch of the border was visited. This ancient custom was repeated every year and the historic procession developed into a pageant. It served to remind the people of their history and traditions and to teach the young men exactly where the boundary markers stood.

Ceremony

Burghs usually had their own seal, as well as robes and chains of office for the chief dignitaries. In full regalia they would ride out to inspect the marches. After Flodden, the Border country was especially keen to uphold its traditions and, in doing so, to pay tribute to the many who fell in battle. Many towns had their charters renewed which included a command to be vigilant in inspecting their boundaries. They devised rituals and appointed townspeople, dressed appropriately, 'in their best equipage' to take part in annual processions. At these they paraded the flag or standard of the burgh and read out the charter with due solemnity and pride.

Fun

After the serious part of the ceremony was over there was time for fun, dancing and feats of skill. Each town tried to outdo the other and this rivalry manifested itself in competitive events such as handball, football, foot-races, horse-races, tugs of war and other sports. In many places, especially outwith the Borders, it is the fun part of the event which has developed into an annual fair or gala but its origins are now forgotten.

LANIMER

Another name for a land boundary was 'landmark', this was corrupted to 'Lanimer' or 'Lanimar' and gave its name to celebrations in places such as Lanark, Rutherglen and Renfrew.

Lanark Lanimer Day

Here the riders in the procession carry a 'birkin bush'; a branch of this sacred wood is traditionally considered to ward off evil. Coins are also thrown into a stream, a survival of a custom favoured by the Druids to pacify the old gods and prevent them taking a life. The date of the Lanark Lanimer is close to that of the old date of Beltane and the customs of those rites have largely fused with those of the ridings. This is further emphasized by the houses and buildings being decked with greenery and by the fools who, dress outrageously and caper alongside the main procession. The bell inscribed with the date 1100 A.D. is tolled to begin the ceremony.

> *I did for thrice three centuries hing,*
> *And unto Lanark city ring.*
>
> Traditonal

Redding the Marches

The Royal Burgh of Rutherglen was proud of its status as one of the earliest burghs. It gained its charter in 1126, but it is now swallowed up by the City of Glasgow, whose charter was granted fifty years later. Each new burgess had to provide a march stone on which was carved his initials. His fellow burgesses carried besoms of broom as well as wearing it on their hats. At the site of the new stone they challenged each other to fight, using the brooms as weapons, to remind them of its position. Rutherglen has revived its Landemark Day in recent years.

Renfrew

In 1904 a decision was made to revive the Riding of the Lanimers so that the younger generation would become familiar with them. The honour of leading the procession on horseback fell to the Provost who, although he agreed with the spirit of revising the Inspection of the Lanimers, declined to carry this out mounted on a horse.

Guid Nychburris

This means 'Good Neighbours' and originated from a court which was held in the Middle Ages where neighbours who had quarrelled were obliged to make up. Guid Nychburris is a festival still held in Dumfries in June. It celebrated the granting of a new Royal Charter to the town, in 1395, by King Robert III and was originally held on Hallowe'en when apples were thrown into the crowd by the Principals. The text of this charter is read out annually. In the 1972 description in the official guide book to the town, it says that the day began early, at seven-thirty, when a courier rode into the town to announce the imminent arrival of the King's Messenger bearing the Charter. The Provost and Town Drummer in turn informed the people and gave the signal for the Cornet to ride out to meet him.

The procession rode out eastwards and took the Messenger with them to inspect the Burgh's boundaries. At ten-thirty the Mid-steeple bell was rung to announce the return of the party and the Charter was presented to the Provost along with the Seal, earth, stone and water. The Queen of the South was crowned as a symbol of the new generation who would continue the tradition. There were fancy-dress parades, sports and entertainments. The day finished with the Beating of the Retreat along the Whitesands, the wide promenade beside the River Nith, and a fireworks display was held.

RIDING THE MARCHES

The celebrations take place often over the period of a week culminating on the Saturday with the actual riding in procession around the boundaries. The principals are also committed to taking part in neighbouring ridings and have other responsibilities to their town throughout their year of office.

Standard bearers
Names
The standard bearer is called by different names in various towns. The most common is 'Cornet'. It is considered to be an honour and when, in 1760, the Cornet at Hawick refused to carry the colour, there was a riot. Usually it is an unmarried young man who should have taken part in previous ridings and be an experienced horseman. In Kelso he is the 'Kelso Lad'. In Moffat, the 'Shepherd', Melrose has its 'Melrosian', Jedburgh its 'Callant', and Galashiels its 'Braw Lad'. In Duns he is the 'Reiver', in Musselburgh, the 'Honest Lad'.

Selection
The person chosen to carry the standard or burgh flag, which nowadays is a replica of the original, is the most important role. He is chosen by a variety of methods. In some places it is by a committee of burgesses in others by nomination from the townspeople. In Kelso it is by a group of ex-Kelso Lads, in Hawick a party of ex-Cornets ride to the home of the new Cornet and summon him to attend at the Town Hall. In Peebles it can be a married man. In a break with a forty-eight year old tradition, as no young man came forward at Duns, in 1996, a girl, originally nominated as the 'Reiver's Lass', was given the honour.

Incorporated Weavers of Selkirk

A standard, the appearance of which bespeaks its antiquity, is still carried annually (on the day of riding their Common) by a

*member of the Corporation of Weavers, in memory of the fact
that it was taken by one of their members from the English on
the field of Flodden.*

Minstrelsy of the Scottish Borders, Walter Scott 1802

Costume

The costumes donned for the occasion are usually in the style
of the eighteenth century. In Hawick, the Cornet wears a tail-
coat of green. In Langholm he has brown gaiters. In nearly all
the ceremonies the principals are presented with sashes to wear
during the proceedings.

Trial runs

Throughout the week there are trial runs which cover certain
routes. In Hawick, should the Cornet complete satifactorily
the climb to Mosspaul, he is awarded membership of the
Ancient Order of Moss Troopers. These were the infamous
cattle reivers of the seventeenth century.

Cornet's reel

The Cornet, or other standard bearer, often hosts a ball. In
Hawick at midnight the Cornets, past and present, take the floor
to dance the Cornet's Reel. In Peebles all the Principals take part.

Principals

Lasses

The standard bearer, whatever his name, has a lass to support
him at ceremonial functions. She is the chief female participant
and is usually a horsewoman. She takes part in the processions,
nowadays riding astride the horse. In Galashiels the 'Braw lass'
has always had equal standing with her 'Braw lad' but in
Hawick no women, traditionally, follow the men out onto the
moor. In 1996 a group of women on horseback gate-crashed the
proceedings and an uproar ensued.

Queens

The crowning of the queen is a popular part of the ceremony in
most towns. In some towns where the riding of the bounds has
become extinct the appointment of a Queen has survived as
part of a gala day. This is a fusion with the rights of May Day
when 'queens of the May' were chosen and crowned and

flowers played a large part in the ceremonies. It was therefore a festival of the return of fertility to the land. Other customs which have remained are floral arches, bonfires and fireworks and dancing round the maypole which takes place at Duns.

Names of Queens

Peebles appoints a Beltane Queen; this ceremony dates from the revival of the Beltane Festival in 1837; Moffat has the Queen of Annandale, Irvine its Marymas Queen – although the occasion is on the day dedicated to the Virgin Mary, the Queen is attired as in the time of Mary, Queen of Scots. Biggar has its Fleming Queen, after the main heritor, Lord Fleming, Annan its Queen of the Border, Dumfries its Queen of the South and Duns its Wynsome Maid. The period of their reign can be a day, a week or a year and during that time they are honoured by the Provost, Magistrates, the local laird and often their Member of Parliament.

Pursuivants and other attendants

Most ridings included a 'pursuivant', or King's Messenger and, or, a courier, a drummer, a lynar whose job it was to learn and trace the boundaries, 'halberdiers' carrying weapons to defend the party and other attendants.

Provosts and Baillies

The Provost, who is also the senior magistrate and his bailllies, the junior magistrates, always played a major part in all civic ceremonies. In the Middle Ages when they went about the town they were treated with great respect. To show their importance they wore hats at all times not bonnets. They had a guard of halberdiers or spearmen. Burgesses doffed their bonnets to them in passing. In many towns these halberdiers were incorporated into the procession. The Provost plays a major part in the ceremonies of the ridings.

Sometimes these civic dignatories were made fun of, as at Hawick in 1850.

> *Deriding, mocking, and scoffing and abusing the said baillies the foresaid day at the riding of the marches.*
> *Hawick Common Riding*, J. Edgar, 1886

Nicht afore the morn

The Friday night of the week of the ridings is always lively. Concerts are often held which include community singing; there are dinners, dances and other entertainments.

Bussing the colours

An important part of the ceremonies, this takes place on the Friday evening when the lass or another invited lady ties the colours to the top of the burgh standard which is carried round the boundaries next morning. It is then placed in the keeping of the standard bearer with the injunction to return it 'unsullied and unstained' after the riding.

Bussing the statues

In Hawick, after the colours are bussed, the procession forms and rides to the statue which commemorates the bravery of the young men who defended the town at Hornshole in 1337 and ties blue and gold ribbons to it. At Moffat the statue of a ram is decorated with heather and bracken at a torchlight procession on the Wednesday evening.

Songs

Througout the ceremonies of the riding of the marches a variety of songs are sung. The most general are 'Scot's Wha Hae', 'The Flowers of the Forest ' and 'Auld Lang Syne' but many were peculiar to one town such as 'The Colours' sung at Hawick.

> *The Colours, the rousing martial Common Riding song. The music dates from the most ancient times and expresses more than any other air the wild defiant strain of the war tramp and the battle shout.*
>
> > *Hawick shall triumph mid destruction,*
> > *Was a Druid's dark prediction;*
> > *Strange the issues that unrolled it,*
> > *Centuries after he'd foretold it.*
> > *Teribus, ye Teri Odin*
> > *Sons of heroes slain at Flodden,*
> > *Imitating Border Bowmen,*
> > *Aye defend your rights and Commons.*
>
> *Ordnance Gazetteer of Scotland*, Francis H. Groome, 1882

At Melrose 'Here's tae Melrose' is sung as well as the 'Melrose Festival Song'. Peebles has its 'Beltane Festival Song', Selkirk folk are wakened at four o'clock in the morning with 'Hail, Smiling Morn' and have as their signature tune 'Up wi' the Soutar's o' Selkirk'. 'The Braw, Braw Lads' is sung at Galashiels, 'Jethart's Here' at Jedburgh and 'Kelsae, Bonnie Kelsae' in Kelso and 'Bonnie Gallowa'' in Galloway.

Proclamations

At most Riding of the Marches ceremonies, part of the original charter of the burgh is read out from the market cross or some important place and other announcements are also made. Some ridings are held on traditional fair days and the Peace of the Fair is proclaimed. At others, the setting up of special March Courts to protect and defend the rights of the burgh were announced.

Crying of the marches

At Linlithgow the Crying of the Marches involved a procession in which the children of the town took a great delight as they chorused, 'Oyez! Oyez!' At Langholm the cry is made with the Town Crier standing on the back of a stout horse.

> *Noo, gentlemen, we're gan frae the Toun,*
> *And first o' a' the Kil-Green we gang roun',*
> *It is an ancient place where clay is got,*
> *And it belangs tae us by Right and Lot;*
> *And then frae there the lang-Wood we gang throu',*
> *Whaur every ane may brecons cut an' pu';*
> *And last o' a' we to the Moss do steer*
> *To see gif a' our marches they be clear;*
> *And when unto the Castle craigs we come,*
> *We'll cry the Langholm Fair,*
> *And then we'll beat the drum.*
>
> Traditional

Crying the Burley

This was a ceremony held in Selkirk , the origin of which was a special court for settling disputes. The Standard bearer is accompanied by four Burleymen to ensure that there is no trouble or interference with the inspection of the march stones.

Their names are called out, or cried, on the Thursday night before the riding.

Fencing the court

The declaration of this, usually made by the Town Crier, to give warning that no-one must molest the officials taking part, is done with ceremony. This protects the Provost and Magistrates while they ride the boundaries and it was called fencing the court. The Court was usually adjourned for another twelve months except in a case of riot.

Slogans

These were the rallying cries from the days when all men capable of carrying arms were expected to keep ready their weapons, a bag of bannocks and a pair of stout shoes in good repair. On hearing the cry they must grab these and run to the traditional gathering place. Many of these slogans were called at the Riding of the Marches. 'A Loreburn! A Loreburn!' was the cry in Dumfries; 'Dae Richt, Fear nocht!,' in Kelso; 'Jethart's Here' in Jedburgh; 'Duns Dings A',' at Duns ; ' Farfar will be Farfar still' in Forfar, and there were many more.

Religious involvement
Relics

Before the Reformation it was traditional that if there were relics, bones, a head, arm or staff of the titular saint of the town, these were carried around the boundaries on the appointed day of the inspection. The Craft Guilds of Edinburgh on September the first, the Feast of St Giles, their patron saint, displayed his relics by parading them in procession through the town. It is believed that relics existed in Coldingham (St Ebba) and Paisley (St Munn), at Tain those of St Duthac which were treated in this way.

After the Reformation Scotland became a mainly Presbyterian country under the General Assembly of the Church of Scotland to which the king or queen must bow. In most towns the Town Council was kirked once a year.

Kirking

On the civic occasion of the Riding of the Marches, the previous

Sunday all the townspeople went to the church where a service was held to Kirk the Cornet, his Lass and all the Principals.

A formal procession would set out and ride in style to the door of the kirk where the Principals and Provost would be received by the minister and escorted into the church.

War memorials

In the midst of the fun and excitement of the day time was taken in many towns to remember those of their kinsmen who fought and died in every war. A halt was made during the procession or a special service held to honour the dead. Usually a wreath was laid. At Innerleithen on St Ronan's Day a service was held when the poem 'For the Fallen' was recited and the Psalm 'I to the Hills will lift mine eyes' sung. This was also the choice at Linlithgow. At Peebles a one minute silence was held. At Jedburgh 'O God our help in ages past' was followed by the 'Last Post' played on a bugle.

Casting the Colours

At Selkirk the last act of the official ceremonies is the Casting of the Colours when the flags are lowered in memory of those who fell at Flodden. The Standard Bearer swirls his flag casting it backwards and forwards reminiscent of the lone survivor bearing the tragic news of the defeat at Flodden in 1513. There is a one-minute silence and the lament, 'The Flowers o' the Forest' is played by the band.

Covenanters

At Duns, during Reiver's Week, a conventicle or open-air service is held. The Reiver places the flag close to the Covenanters' Stone and Psalms are sung as they were in the days of 'The Preachings' when those Presbyterians who refused to sign the 'Test', an oath of loyalty to the king and the Episcopalian church, had to take to the hills as outlaws or be killed. The Covenanters are also remembered in Biggar.

Processions

These were the highlight of the Ridings. In most towns there were several processions during the week. A great variety of customs could be seen.

Sod and stone
The ritual of collecting earth and stone is one which appears in many accounts of ridings. The earth, stone and often also water were symbolic of the lands and streams within the boundaries.

Mixed marriage
In Galashiels the Braw Lad and Lass ride in procession on the Wednesday night to Torwoodlee, the home of the Pringles, the main landowners, and ask permission to cut a turf from the land and take a stone from the old tower, then they carry these back into the town. At a later ceremony on the Saturday the Braw Lass places them at the foot of the Market Cross along with a bunch of thistles and a mixed bunch of red and white roses. These represent the marriage of Margaret Tudor of England to King James IV of Scotland in 1503.

Turf-cutter
Musselburgh appointed a Turf-Cutter who wore a special uniform of green. This personage, accompanied by his own squire, the Town Champion and his squires and a lawyer – or as he was called a Notary Public – set out to visit the march stones on the 'Nicht afore the morn'. At each point the Turf-Cutter would cut a sod, toss it up in the air and call out 'Its a' oor ain'.

Hawick
At a point where three lands meet the Cornet cuts a sod to remember the meaning of the Common Rights. These were given in the original charter 'for peats and pasture, land for tillage' to the people for all time.

Box and Flaggon bearers
'Lynars' are appointed at Dumfries. They trace the boundaries and also carry home earth to symbolize the extent of the Burgh land. This is collected at each march point and placed in a special box; a flaggon of water is drawn from the River Nith which symbolizes the rivers and burns which flow through the town.

Duns
At Duns, the Reiver, representing the 'feuars', the descendants of the lairds who were given feus by the Abbey to which the

charter was originally given, uses a spade decorated with the town's colours to ceremoniously cut a sod from the Common.

Torchlight

There are several torchlight processions held. At Duns, over one thousand bearers come to the Cross from various directions carrying blazing torches. These are paraded through the town to the Public Park where they are thrown onto a bonfire. This is followed by a firework display. At Moffat a torchlight procession is held on the Wednesday evening which arrives at the Ram from various directions. From there the Shepherd and his Lass lead the way to Hope-Johnston Park where a bonfire is lit and fireworks end the festivities.

Boundary ceremonies

Ceremonies were often held to encourage the people to place firmly in their minds the position of the boundary markers. There were three divisions which marked out boundaries. One was headroom, which was the termination of the town on the summit of a hill, the second was the line of hills between two glens and the third water, be it sea, river, stream or loch. In early disputes proof of a boundary was given by rolling away the march stone as underneath it the ground should have been burnt and the ashes should remain.

Hole in the hedge

At Annan during the Sunday morning procession a halt is made at Langlands where they are met by the Provost and Magistrates and a small boy is pushed through a hole in the hedge accompanied by a skelp from the Provost where the boy touches an old landmark to impress its whereabouts on his mind.

White paint

At Newburgh in Fife the Town's Officer daubs each of the boundary stones with white paint.

Snuffing

This is another short ceremony held at Annan when the Provost and Town Clerk offer the Burgh snuff box round the company, both mounted and on foot. They are invited to take a sniff for good luck.

Wild plum leaves

In Galashiels the company halt at the Raid Stane where sprigs of wild plums are distributed in honour of the 'Soor Plum' incident of 1337 when the English soldiers who were camping near the confluence of the Gala and Tweed rivers were attacked and chased off by the men of Gala. The men returned to the town waving branches of wild plum trees to announce their victory.

Elgin

At Elgin the Convenor of the Trades taps the boundary stone three times with his ceremonial staff.

Trysting tree

Kelso has a Whipmans Procession as well as the main riding. It halts at the place where the original 'trysting' or meeting tree stood where there is now just a post to mark the spot. Here the Whipman cuts his initials on the ground. They should be carved so that someone reading them realizes the direction in which the procession has gone. This was a custom used by the Borderers during raids as a signal to their followers.

> *In the Parish of Linton, Roxburghshire there is a circle of stones, surrounding a smooth plot of turf, called the Tryst; or place of appointment, which tradition avers to have been the rendezvous of neighbouring warriors. The name of the leader was cut in the turf and the arrangement of letters announced to his followers the course which he had taken.*
> Parish of Linton, Statistical Account of Scotland, 1796

Ducking

To remind those Burghers of Lanark who had not previously ridden the marches of the whereabouts of the boundaries, a stop was made at the Ducking-Hole and they were immersed in the water. Coins were thrown into the water of the River Mouse and were retrieved by the children.

Cairns

At Lauder the Cornet places a stone on the Burgess Cairn which marks the boundary of the highest point of the ride.

Dumping

Town Councillors at Sanquhar suffered the ignominy of being 'dumped' on the Dumping Stone which marks the boundaries. This has taken place at Bauldie's Burn since the Burgh Charter, granted by James III, in 1484, has been read by the Chaplain. A similar fate awaited a new Burgess of Aberdeen where he was 'douped' on being admitted a Free Burgess; this took place during a ceremony, after the Court was fenced at Weather Craig during the Riding of the Landimars.

Monks and minstrels

The Masonic Lodge of Melrose was founded almost nine hundred years ago by the masons who built the Abbey. At Newstead, the site of the original Lodge, a representative carrying a mallet meets the Melrosian and his party from the town of 'monks and minstrels'.

Water

The crossing of rivers and streams by leaping them on horseback, fording them and crossing over bridges plays a part in many of the processions.

Mementoes

A reminder of their service during their time of office was given to many of those taking part in the annual proceedings. At Kelso, a small dagger of the kind worn by the Kirk Yetholm gypsies was presented to the Kelso Laddie. In several burghs it was an engraved riding crop. At Elgin the convenor of the inspection receives samples of the work of the various crafts from members of the Craft Guild.

Weapons

Up until the eighteenth century it was common for weapons to be carried in earnest at all times in case of attack. The Borderers even went armed to social occasions.

> After the enclosure of the burgh lands the warlike nature of
> the proceedings slowly disappeared, and the practice of riding
> the marches armed was discontinued about the close of the
> last century. The two glittering halberds carried by the burgh

officers being now the only remnant of the once imposing military display.

Hawick Common Riding, J. Edgar, 1886

Food and drink

Food and drink are a part of all occasions on which the marches are inspected. During the common ridings several dinners are held at which an ex-patriot usually makes a speech and proposes a toast. However there are also rituals concerning food and drink which are an inherent part of the ceremonies of riding the marches and which vary from place to place.

Blackness milk

The procession at Linlithgow halted first at the Bridge Inn for a loving cup to be passed around and then at the house of the baron-baillie to receive a glass of Blackness milk which was always laced with whisky. The day began here with a series of breakfasts laid on by the Provost and the Dyers Society.

Whisky and cake

At Lauder the Lauderdale Hunt join in the procession at the Waterin Stane where tables are set out with cake, wine and whisky for toasts. This was also on offer at Eaglesham.

Mead

Mead has been made for centuries from honey bees kept by the monks at Melrose Abbey. A gift of honey is offered to the Melrosian by the Abbot in exchange for the traditional gift of wax for making candles. Fruit and wine are offered to the company.

Mutton feast

At Gilmerton they sat down to a mutton feast in the Friendly Society Hall; at Newburgh it was mutton pies and beer, while at Forfar the traditional bridie was served along with cheese, bannocks, kale and clootie dumpling.

Baps

At Musselburgh bread rolls or baps were handed over as part of the ceremony. These had three mussel shells embedded on them as a symbol of the fishing industry.

Parades, Processions and Pageants

*A*ttendances at festivals and processions was compulsory for all Crafts Guilds in pre-Reformation times, each Craft marching in its appointed order, its members bearing or carrying the tokens and banners of their craft. All processionists had to wear green coats. Parades and processions remained popular throughout Scotland and every town and village had at least one every year while larger towns and cities would hold several. Most were made up of a variety of groups – the Civic dignitaries, the incorporated guilds of trades and craftsmen and the friendly societies with their banners flying took part. The local volunteer company or Rifle Volunteers, the Masonic Lodge, local bands, youth organizations and in some areas the local firms often joined in.

Carts, and later lorries, would be decorated, a prize often being given for the best. Children followed in fancy-dress and the whole town would be decorated with flags and bunting.

Sports were held and fairground shows and stalls would be set up.
Usually these were annual events however sometimes they were
put on for a special occasion such as the laying of the foundation
stone of a public building or to celebrate a public event such as
a coronation, jubilee, centenary or the ending of a war.

The Relief of Mafeking

*The rejoicings started at 6 a.m. Anyone going down to the
Yard gate at that time on Saturday morning would have seen
thousands of workmen congregated there . . . It was the first time
that they had heard of the long-looked for Relief of Mafeking
. . . Pipes were speedily commandeered . . . flags seemed to leap
from space, and in a short time all Clydebank was in a whirl of
excitement as the processionists gaily marched citywards . . .*

*After breakfast the fun grew fast and furious . . . Works with
flags, houses with flags, bairns with flags, staid domestic men
with flags, demure young ladies with flags, coalmen with flags,
hawkers with flags . . . The telephone men fixed a Royal
Standard to the top of one of their poles. In two four-in-hand
brakes . . . .apprentices paraded the Burgh led by one of them
on a charger dressed as Baden-Powell. When Singer closed at
11 o'clock they swelled the numbers carrying in front of them
an effigy of Kruger . . . which was later burned.*

Clydebank Press, 25th May 1900

Fisher Folk

The fisher community have always celebrated festivals in their
own way. There were three fishing seasons – Doon-drawin' at
Beltane, Johnsmas in Midsummer, and Lammas – at which
foys, farewell feasts, were held. In addition there were herring
queens, fishermen's walks and fairs.

Fishermen's Walks
Musselburgh

*At an early hour on Friday the New Street of Fisherrow,
principally inhabited by the fishing population, presented a very
animated appearance. The fishermen are wont to celebrate their
return from the herring-fishing by an annual procession, and the
day is set apart by them as a high holiday. The procession was*

*headed by the band of the 5th Midlothian Rifle Volunteers,
and with flags flying, left New Street a little before three
o'clock, and marched by Fisher's Wynd and High Street to
Bridge Street, where they halted in front of the residence of
Provost Lawrie, who kindly treated them to cakes and wine.
After giving three ringing cheers for the Provost and his lady,
the fishermen proceeded by the High Street, past the Town
Hall, and along the Newbigging to Inveresk, returning about
half-past four o' clock by the same route to their homes. The
procession was accompanied part of the way by a number of
young fisher-women in their everyday attire, and following the
band came the old and middle-aged men in their pea jackets
and Sunday hats and bringing up the rear were the able-bodied
young men – in all about 100. The whole party conducted
themselves in a most orderly manner.*

North British Agriculturalist, 28th September 1867

Box-Meeting Day

This was the name given to the festival held on the third Friday
in September in Cockenzie and Port Seton. The herring fleet
had returned from the summer fishing and this was celebrated
with a parade or walk. The Fishermen and girls, for there were
many girls, followed the herring fleet in teams of two gutters
and a packer, around the ports as far south as Yarmouth. The
Friendly Society's members paraded their banner and symbols
of office including their 'box' into which people put offerings
to be used to help the sick and needy. A Boxmaster and his
Three Key men led the parade. They wore their striking
costumes and were led by a band. A bonfire had been lit and
fireworks had been set off the previous evening on the Boat
Shore. The villages were decorated with bunting and a dance
rounded off the day.

Herring Queens

In fishing ports the Herring Queen festivals are popular in the
same way that the crowning of the local Gala Queen takes
place in rural communities. It was originally a celebration of
the return of the herring fleet when walks and picnics took
place.

In Wick and Eyemouth the Herring Queen and her maids were chosen by the fishing community and every local skipper nominated a girl to be a member of the Queen's Court. A ballot took place to decide which boat would have the honour of carrying the Queen into harbour on its deck. All the boats were decorated with flags and an escort of boats accompanied that of the Queen. The local lifeboats also took part. The Queen, in Eyemouth, was dressed in blue velvet with silver net which is a symbol of the sea while at Wick she was dressed in silver blue and green. In Eyemouth her Maids of Honour formed a pattern of the points of the compass and were also dressed in herring net decorated with silver ribbons. They carried bread, fruit and corn as symbols of plenty. Flower girls wearing rainbow-coloured dresses joined in the procession and carried flowers. Their capes were also in silver net. The boys were represented in Eyemouth by three white-clad sailors and in Wick by green and silver clad riders who escorted the Queen's carriage. In Eyemouth the Queen distributed awards for the largest catch at the end of the week of celebrations. The ceremony ended with the singing of the hymn 'Eternal Father Strong to Save'. In both there were races and fun-fairs and dances.

Burrymen

In the middle ages it was thought that evil could cling to the skin like burrs. The Burryman was someone who was blamed for the bad luck of a fishing season or community. In many ports in the North-East it was believed that if he was chased out of the village things would improve. In Buckie, when the fishing was poor they dressed a fisherman in a flannel shirt and stuck burrs, the seed heads of the burdock, to it before wheeling him through the town in a barrow in an attempt to drive the bad luck away. In Fraserburgh, in 1864, they decorated a man with burrs and red herrings, sat him on a horse and piped him through the town but there was no improvement to the fishing.

South Queensferry

The Burryman here was paraded, in August, fully covered from head to toe in burrs and with a crown of roses. He carried two staves covered in flowers. The procession covered the boundaries of the town. At every stop the Burryman was greeted and showered with gifts of money which went into the collecting can of his attendants. The young men who are the main participants share the spoils between them to spend at the Ferry Fair. Not everyone saw this as harmless fun:

Injurious to morals of those who only require excitement to indulge in intemperance.

First Statistical Account of Scotland, 1796

Farmers
Horse and Plough Festival
In Orkney children dressed up as horses and ploughmen at Eastertime. The youngest children wore fancy costumes with pearly harnesses and splendid tails and acted as horses. Sometimes they painted their shoes to look like horseshoes. Those boys over ten were ploughmen. A miniature ploughing match was held on the sands where markings were drawn out where they had to make furrows. Long ago these would be a cow's hoof attached to a stick but later, smiddy-made model ploughs became fashionable and are now collectors' pieces. The day continued with games and dancing.

Farmers' Parade
At Kilwinning there was a Farmers' Parade held at the local fair in July. A Captain and Colonel were appointed. They paraded on horseback with the horses' harnessess gaily decorated. They wore hats adorned with flowers and ribbons and new shot oats. Across their breasts they wore showy satin sashes. A large flag was carried and the parade was led by a band and a piper. Afterwards there was a horse-race.

Carters and Whipmen
The parades which were held by the Carters were called Plays, meaning holidays or fetes where races and fun, picnics and dancing took place. They were mainly held in rural areas and were based on the Societies of Carters, later Whipmen which were formed to provide welfare benefits to those of this calling who fell sick or to their families if they should die.

Marymas Fair

At Irvine since the Middle Ages, every August, the Marymas Fair was held. This was organized by the Society of Cadgers. This was the original name of the Society of Carters. The Captain of the Carters' Society was the principal figure and had a right-hand and left-hand man, who represented Wallace and Bruce. The Procession of the Brothered Carters assembled at the house of the ex-Captain and they journeyed to the house of the Captain-elect to convey him to the meeting place. They visited the original gates or ports of entry to the town and arrived at a specially erected platform outside the Town House, at noon. Here they were welcolmed by the Provost and Baillies. The Queen was accompanied by her Four Maries and was dressed in the costume of the time of Mary, Queen of Scots. She was escorted by the Captain.

The flags were bussed with ribbons before the Procession rode out to the Town Moor which was gifted to Irvine by Robert the Bruce. Halberdiers, axemen and banner-bearers all on horseback, joined the procession. In the afternoon games and races took place.

Gilmerton

A Boxmaster was appointed at Gilmerton where the Play Society was established in 1787. Originally the contributions were paid in pins which were sold and the money was added to the Box. The members wore royal blue sashes and the procession began at the Friendly Society Hall. The Brothered Carters decorated their horses' harnesses with ribbons and flowers.

> *The riders looked for all the world like haberdashery shops. Great bunches of wallflower, thyme, spearmint, bachelor buttons, gardner's gartens, peony roses, gillyflower and southernwood were stuck in their buttonholes, and broad belts of striped silk, of every colour in the rainbow, were flung across their shoulders*
>
> Mansie Waugh, D.M. Moir, 1828

Dancing took place in the streets – this was called a jing-a-ring and started as a small circle which grew and grew as more people joined in. The fun went on until the following morning.

West Linton

Members of any trade which used a whip could join the Whipman's Friendly Society. In West Linton the Society, which included those from the surrounding area, held an annual parade. This through time became formalized and a Whipman was selected who had a Lass and a Barony Herald, a younger boy. In the second week of June the ceremony of installation took place on the Friday evening and a fancy-dress parade was also held. Sashes are worn and the Whipman's Flag was bussed with colourful ribbons.

> Come Linton folk, lay by your care,
> Tak pleasure's airm and join the fair;
> Let shouts of welcome rend the air,
> In greeting to your Whipman
>> Traditional

The Whipman's Reel is danced at the end of the parade and the day closes with a dinner and ball.

Penicuik

A Huntsman and his Lass were installed at Penicuik, in June, on the day which originally was the procession or Walk of the Friendly Societies.

Boys' Walk

On New Year's Day in Dufftown the young boys who were members of the Juvenile Society of the Distillers' Mutual Benefit Association paraded through the streets headed by a pipe band. Girls were later allowed to become members. Money was collected in cans for the refreshments and entertainment at the Boys' Ball.

Craft Guilds

The craft guilds who were very powerful in the Scottish Burghs held annual processions. Originally these were held on the Feast day of their patron, usually a saint. These guilds had splendidly embroidered banners and also had heraldic shields and halberds. Some of the processions took place at night and were torchlit. Shoemakers, hammermen, weavers, tailors, furriers, goldsmiths, saddlers and butchers had their guilds. Deacons were appointed, and the 'Gild Merchant' was a very important personage in a town in the fifteenth century.

Weavers

Volunteers from the the Weavers' Society of Govan, now part of Glasgow, carried their flag at the Battle of Sherrifmuir in 1715. The first Friday in June was the annual Weavers' Parade as well as being the day of the Govan Fair. The band serenaded the retiring Deacon of the Society and the new Deacon was installed at the Mercat Cross. The members then went in procession around the boundaries. The main feature of this procession was a Sheep's Head, a ram complete with horns. A ship's joiner usually had the honour of carrying it. One legend gives an explanation of their choice of emblem. A young man was supposed to have been in love with the local minister's servant lass. The minister forbade them to marry so they eloped but not before the groom took his revenge by decapitating all the minister's flock. The local folk sympathized with their plight and purloined one of the sheep's heads which they had stuffed and mounted. A Gala Queen was added later and her sceptre is topped by a model of a sheep's head.

Aberdeen

The apprentices and servants held a procession on New Year's Day.

King Crispin

The shoemakers, who were known as 'cordiners' (also cordovans or cordwainers), had St Crispin as their patron saint. After the banning of Saints Days in 1581 he was translated into King Crispin and rode in Edinburgh in the procession in a golden targe, or coach accompanied by a colourful retinue which included the Black Prince. A mock coronation took place at Holyrood.

St Obert's Play

St Obert was the patron saint of bakers. At Perth, on December the tenth on the Eve of St Obert a torchlight procession was held in his honour.

The bakers of that city were accustomed to pass through the streets in procession by torchlight, playing pipes and beating

*drums, and wearing various disguises. One of their number used
to wear a dress known as The Devil's Coat. Another rode on a
horse shod with men's shoes. In its primitive form this pastime
was probably some kind of sacred drama representing the chief
features in the life of the saint; but its character had changed
in the course of time.*

*On account of their connections with the faith such
performances gave offence to the Puritans. In 1581 'an act
against idolatrous and superstitious pastimes, especially
against Sanct Obert's Play' , was issued by the Session. It
seems to have had little effect, for again in 1587 the bakers
were required 'to take order for the amendment of blasphemous
and heathenish plays of St Obert's pastime.' Eventually in
1588, several 'insolent young men' were imprisoned for their
'idolatrous pastime in playing of Sanct Obert's play, to the
great grief of the conscience of the faithful and infamous
slander of the hail congregation.'*

A *Calendar of Scottish Saints*, Dom Michael Barrett, 1919

Eventually the Bakers' Guild were forced to act against their
members for taking part in the play. It was recorded in their
records in 1588 that anyone disobeying the order would not be
allowed the privileges of the craft and would be banished from the
town *'sin die'* – without limit of time. This had the required effect.

Fertility
Feast of St Nicholas
From 1450, on May the ninth, the Feast Day of St Nicholas, the
Faculty of the University of Glasgow held a procession and
banquet when all Masters, Licentiates, Bachelors and students,
after hearing matins in the Chapel of St Thomas the Martyr,
rode in solemn and stately procession, bearing flowers and
branches of trees, through the public streets from the upper
part of the town to the cross, and so back to the College of the
Faculty; housed at Rottenrow, and there 'amid the joy of the
feast' they toasted the welfare of the faculty.

St Andrews
On May Day at St Andrews University students and staff rode
on horseback, disguised and carrying shields, sceptres and

swords. Their horses were decorated with greenery and this may have been a throwback to the Pagan fertility festival which carried the spirit of fertility throughout the town.

Culross

> *At Culross a custom prevailed from time immemorial for young men to perambulate the streets in procession, carrying green boughs, on the first of July each year. The Town Cross was decorated with garlands and ribbons, and the procession would pass several times round it before disbanding to spend the day in amusements.*
>
> A Calendar of Scottish Saints, Dom Michael Barrett, 1919

This was done in honour of its titular saint, St Serf, on his feast day.

PALM SATURDAY

> *A gala kept by the boys of the Grammar School, beyond all memory in regard to date, on the Saturday before Palm Sunday. They then parade the streets with a Palm or its substitute, a large tree of the willow kind, 'salix caprea', ornamented with daffodils, mezeron, and box-tree. This day is called Palm Saturday, and the custom is certainly a Popish relic of very ancient standing.*
>
> Parish of Lanark, First Statistical Account of Scotland, 1795

A similar custom appears to have taken place in Moray.

Commissioner's Walk

Every year, in May, the General Assembly of the Church of Scotland is held in Edinburgh. The Lord High Commissioner, representing the Monarch, drives from Holyrood Palace to the General Assembly Hall, at the top of the Lawnmarket accompanied by civic dignatories, 'distinguished persons' and a military escort to the opening of the Assembly.

Pageants

Tableaux of an amazingly spectacular nature were staged at pageants in honour of royalty, of towns and especially to reproduce historic events. Many towns stage these annually to celebrate a memorable date in their history. The Church of Rome allotted to every craft guild a patron saint. Every guild celebrated its Saint's Day with a pageant.

Royalty

Edinburgh enjoyed staging pageants on state occasions. The fountains ran with red and white wine. Triumphal arches were decorated with flowers and other greenery as were the platforms which were set up and on which elaborate set-pieces were arranged. The platform at the Tron was daubed with clay and decorated with woodbine and jonets, or yellow flowers, which were embedded in it. In 1558 a tree was erected with two dozen tennis balls covered with gold tinsel and hundreds of cherries. Seven dancers with thirty-one dozen bells attached to their clothes, some dressed in red, others in white, performed. The account books show that the City Fathers provided them with a cart to take them from one stage to another, a guard to keep the crowd back, a house where they dressed and for the food and drink supplied to them there.

Mary, Queen of Scots

An elaborate pageant was staged for the entry of Mary, Queen of Scots in 1561. Children took part, as they often did, and sang like angels. A beautiful child appeared from out of a cloud and gave the Queen the keys to the City and a bound Bible. The cavalcade which accompanied her dressed as Moors in black and yellow. The principal men were dressed in purple velvet and taffeta and everyone wore jewels.

Entry into Edinburgh of Princess Anne of Denmark

In 1590, Anne of Denmark, bride of James VI arrived by the West Port. She was greeted with triumph and great joy. Pageants, as the tableaux platforms were called, were erected. Young boys with artificial wings flew towards her and presented her with two silver keys to the City of Edinburgh. Guns were fired in salute.

Forty-two young men in white taffeta and cloth of silver with gold chains disguised as Moors, danced before her along the streets. At the tolbooth, 'younkers', as young noblemen were called, dressed in women's clothing and represented peace, plenty, justice, liberality and temperance; Bacchus and the goddess of corn and wine caused the fountains to flow with claret which spilled over onto the causeway. Seven planets were depicted at the Nether Bow and children with branches depicted her family tree. The words were spoken in Latin as she did not understand English.

Kate Kennedy
Lady Katherine Kennedy is represented at this annual pageant at St Andrews University by a first-year student or 'bejan'. The setting is medieval, the costumes a variety of styles. Historical figures from the archives of the university and from Scottish history are represented. The procession tours the town and returns to the grounds of the university. Chauvinism reigns, it is an all-male show. Originally this was held at Candlemas, a popular time for university rag days. It is now held in April but still collects for charity.

Arbroath
The Abbot and his bishops were represented at the ruins of Arbroath Abbey in a floodlit pageant which told of its turbulent history. They even threatened the Pope if he would not heed their *Declaration of Arbroath*, the Declaration of the Independence of Scotland, endorsed by King Edward II of England in 1328. King Robert the Bruce rode at the head of the procession through the town. The fishing community joined in and the celebrations lasted for a week.

Lilias Day
St Barchan was the titular saint of Kilbarchan and the third Saturday in August was his Feast day. Originally a fair was held at Beltane and it is reputed that in 1704 William Cuninghame substituted his daughter's name, which was Lilias, in place of the 'heathen title of Beltane Queen'. She was a relative of the Glencairns, the land superiors, when Kilbarchan was raised to a Burgh of Barony in 1704. Through time both celebrations were incorporated into Lilias Day and commemorated by a pageant.

Fairs and Foys

FAIRS

*F*airs were originally serious gatherings which were legally permitted under a royal charter granted by the king. The number of fairs and the number of days over which they should be held was laid down by law. They were the main places for buying and selling goods and services. They were often under the jurisdiction of the local laird or, in cities, of the incorporated trades guilds. There were several types of fair and a variety of dates which differed in every part of the country.

There were Holy Fairs, which were in reality the Sacramental Fast days on which communion was celebrated in the open air by ministers of the Church of Scotland; horse fairs where the gypsies congregated to buy and sell horses, cattle fairs and trysts, and feeing fairs at which farm workers and servants could find a new position and farmers could hire hands.

There were fairs which specialized in certain items such as lintseed, scythes, wool, whelks, puddings, curds, crockery and many other goods, others were for the sale of lambs, sheep or breeds of cattle and bulls.

As shops became a permanent feature of most villages and travel became easier between towns, the importance of the fairs, except for the sale of livestock, dwindled. Many retained their 'shows', as the carnival aspect was known, and several are active till this day.

> *Being the only market in the year* [at Kirkdandie] *for the parishes of Girvan, Barr, Ballantrae, Colmonell, Straiton and Dailly, it was numerously attended. Booths and stands were erected for the entertainment of the gathered throng and the disposal of merchandise, which, as there were no roads, was chiefly brought on horseback. Here, those travelling merchants, whose avocation, like Othello's is now gone, but who before communications with the towns came to be so freely opened up, formed nearly the sole medium of sale or barter among the rural population, assembled in great numbers, bringing with them tempting wares of England and the Continent . . . The bivouac of the pedlars with their pack horses, who generally arrived the night before the fair, the bustle of active preparation by earliest dawn, and the gradual gathering of the plaided and bonneted population, from the various pathways across the hills or down the straths, as the day advanced.*
>
> *Tales and Traditions of Scotland*, Andrew Glass, 1878

Number of days

Fairs could last from one to fifteen days and were looked forward to by the ordinary people with great excitement as they were a break from the monotony of everyday life, an excuse to have a holiday, to get dressed up and to meet new people. Preparations would start long before the actual day.

Outsiders

While burgesses and freemen were granted the right to trade at a local fair others known as unfree men could not and had to be granted the right to stalls which were often on the opposite side of the street from the burgesses. Many who took part in the fairs travelled from place to place and had long journeys on very poor roads. They set out with their horse-drawn carts, caravans, strings of horses with panniers on their backs or even on foot, laden with whatever goods were their speciality and set up their booths or traded from a tray carried around their neck ready to receive custom. Cattle and other livestock would be driven along the roads to reach the market-place. A baker, the only one in Dumfries, in 1735, made bread rolls of coarse flour, chiefly bran, which he carried in creels for twenty-seven miles to fairs at Urr and Kirkpatrick.

Foreign merchants

There were, at some fairs, merchants from the Continent of Europe. At the Senzie Market held at St Andrews, for fifteen days at Eastertime, the *Second Statistical Account of Scotland* (1835) reports that there were two to three hundred vessels in the harbour from abroad. At Inveraray at an area dubbed Frenchfarland, merchants from France docked their ships and traded wine for barrels of herring.

Craftsmen

Especially at fairs held in Royal burghs in the fourteenth century there would be many craftsmen, tanners selling leather goods, lorimers selling bits for horses, hammermen who forged swords, cobblers who made and repaired shoes, furriers selling cloaks and hoods of fur, tailors taking orders for suits and dresses and weavers selling cloth as well as the more usual trades.

Packmen

These men toured around the farmtowns all year round bringing information and gossip as well as selling ribbons and laces amongst other items. They often were found at the fairs with their goods laid out on display on the ground. Many of them had lively personalities. Others started as packmen but rose to be merchants often adopting airs and graces above, what those who had known them in former times considered, their station.

One popular song describes the courting of one of the laird o' Glenneuk's daughters by a packman. He threatens her that if she marries her 'He sall get her as bare as the birk-tree at Yule.' However, in this case, it is the packman who has the last laugh.

They were lawfully spliced by the Rev'rend J.P.,
Whilk the hale kintra roun in the 'Herald' may see;
Now his big shop's weel stow'd, baith for bed an' for back,
That was started wi' ballads an' trumps in his pack

He raise up in rank an' he raise up in fame,
An' the title o' Baillie's affixed to his name;
Now the laird o' Glenneuk aboot naething will crack
Save the baillie – but ne'er hints a word o' the pack.

The Pedlar, Vagabond Songs and Ballads, Robert Ford, ed., 1904

On seeing a fair at Inverness one traveller wrote:

In one part the poor women, maid-servants and children, in the
coldest weather, in the dirt and snow, either walking or standing
to talk with one another, without stockings and shoes. In another
place, you see a man dragging along a half-starved horse little
bigger than an ass in a cart about the size of a wheel barrow . . .
the load in this cart, if compact, might be carried under his
arm; but he must not bear any burden himself, though his wife
has, perhaps, a greater load on her loins than he has in his cart.
I say on her loins for the women carry fish, and other heavy
burdens, in the same manner as the Scots pedlars carry their
packs in England . . . Here are four or five fairs a year, when the
Highlanders bring their commodities to market; but good God!
you could conceive that there was misery in this island. One has
under his arm a small roll of linen, another a piece of coarse
plaiding; these are considerable dealers. But the merchandise of
the greatest part of them is of a most contemptible value, such
as these, viz. – two or three cheeses, of about three or four
pounds weight a-piece; a kid, sold for sixpence or eightpence at
the most; a small quantity of butter in something that looks like
a bladder, and is sometimes set down in the dirt in the street;
three or four goatskins; a piece of wood for an axle-tree to one
of the little carts. With the produce of what each of them sells
they generally buy something. A horn, or wooden spoon or two,
a knife, a wooden platter, and such like necessities for their
huts, and carry home with them little or no money.

Letters From the North, Captain Burt, 1735

Islanders

At Greenock the boats would come from the Western Isles and
the islanders would live aboard them during the time of the fair.
They brought webs of cloth, kegs of butter, Highland cattle,
red deer skins, furs of rabbits and pine martens which they

traded for corn, meal and indigo, the dye of the blue madder plant, which they used in their cloth.

Chap books and broadsheets

Chap books were the popular novelettes of their day. They were often 'near the bone' but they were greatly sought after and were on sale at fairs as well as being peddled around the farmtouns and houses by chapmen. Dougal Graham, of Glasgow, a chapman and printer to trade wrote and distributed such gems as 'Paddy from Cork', 'Jocky and Maggie's Courtship' and 'The Remarkable Life and Transactions of Alexander Hamwinkle, heckler, Dancing-master and Ale-seller in Glasgow now Banished for Coining' or 'The Ravishing Dying Words of Christina Ker, Who Died at the Age of Ten'. In addition to these the words and music of ballads such as 'Jockey to the Fair' or 'The Bonnie lass o' Fyvie' were hawked in broadsheet form and were very popular.

Dates

Fairs were held in towns and villages, often on the date which had been the feast day of the saint to whom the original local church had been dedicated. In many areas the names of fairs, by the nineteenth century, were corruptions of these saints' names. Sam Maneuke's Fair, held at Stevenston, Ayrshire in October was a version of St Monoch; Brux Day, held at Millport, Isle of Cumbrae in July was St Brioc; Trewell Fair, held at St Andrews, Fife in October was St Rule and Trodlin's Fair, held at Rescobie, Forfar in October was St Triduana.

Quarter days

Other dates on which fairs were held were the quarter days, Candlemas, February the second; Whitsun, May the twenty-fifth; Lammas, August the first; and Martinmas, November the eleventh. These were also term days in Scotland when rent and accounts were due to be paid.

National saints days

There were national Saints Days on which many fairs were held. These were originally Holy Days when mass was said so they were given the name of the saint with 'mas' added.

Andrew	Anermas\Andermas	30th November
Columba	Colmsmas	2nd June
Fergus	Fergusmas	18th November
George	Georgemas	23rd April
John the Baptist	Johnsmas	24th June
Luke	Lukemas	18th October
Magnus	Magnusmas	16th April
Margaret	Margaretmas	16th November
Martin	Martinmas	11th November
Michael	Michaelmas	29th September
Patrick	Patrickmas	17th March
Peter	Petermas	29th June
Virgin Mary	Marymas	15th August

King James VI banned the holding of feasts on Saints Days in 1651.

Fun and games

After the main business was conducted there was always a great deal of drinking, fun and frolic. Courting, dancing, sports, foot-races and horse-races were indulged in as well as fortune telling, which was prohibited, though often carried on under the disguise of a legitimate trade.

Peace of the Fair

This was the name given to the special protection granted to merchants and traders travelling to and from the fairs in the fifthteenth and sixteenth centuries. It was proclaimed from the market cross by the bellringer and was known as Cryin' the Fair. Anyone breaking the peace by fighting or stealing was banished from the area and never allowed to return. The peace of the fair of Glasgow was proclaimed in the name of the king and the Earl of Lennox, and the baillies, and those frequenting it were enjoined to forget, 'auld dett, new dett, auld feid or new feid', members of crafts' guilds were fined £100 (Scots) equal to £8 sterling for causing disturbances and they were banished from the town. Sometimes a special court was held to deal with any lawbreakers. One special dispensation was allowed at fairtime, – no criminal, runaway or serf (as miners often were in Scotland) could be arrested if found at a fair.

Crying of the fair

A similar cry is used in both Langholm and Lockerbie:

This is to let ye a' ken that there is to be a Muckle fair in ye toun o' Lockerby this day. Whaur gif there be ony land-loupers, horse-coupers, or gang-the-gate daunderers wha sall kick up any rabblement, babblement or squabblement, he sall be nailed by the lug, wi' a twapenny nail, tae the thief's muckle post till a' the bluid's sweeled oot o' him. God save the Queen thrice and the laird o' the soil yince!

Traditional

Fairkeepers

These were one or more men appointed to keep an eye on the behaviour of the crowd,

A group of tradesmen belonging to the town was usually formed into a guard to preserve order and tranquillity. They were called fairkeepers.

History of Kilmarnock, A. McKay, 1888

In Glasgow,

Twenty men of the merchant rank, and two from each craft, each armed with corselet and pike, were elected to keep the peace of the burgh on Fair Saturday . . . and citizens were ordered to put off their accustomed armour on that day.

History of Glasgow, George MacGregor, 1881

Donnybrooks

In the nineteenth century the strict laws were relaxed resulting in several fairs becoming known for the settling of feuds by physical force. It was possible for fifty to a hundred men to struggle against each other with fists or sticks.

The Roitfair, held at the east end of the Parish of Campsie became notorious in the nineteenth century for brawling and quarrelling between the parishioners of Campsie, Kirkintilloch and Kilsyth. The traditional St Machan's Fair, held at Clachan of Campsie in September was transferred by the sheriff to the Newtown at Lennoxtown and held on the day of the Roitfair in October to try to prevent these outbursts of local rivalry.

At Gifford, East Lothian there were regular complaints because every Monday during harvest feeing fairs were held.

> *This had been a great nuisance to the parish, as the shearers*
> *to the number of 500 flock to Gifford on the Sabbath, and not*
> *only wait to be hired, but profane the Lord's Day by drunken*
> *and disorderly conduct.*
>
> Parish of Gifford, *Second Statistical Account of Scotland*, 1835

At the Colm's Day Fair held at Largs, Ayrshire, on June the second, crowds came from the Western Highlands and Islands on the previous night and their celebrations often ended in riots. At the Rood Day Fair in Jedburgh Thomas Kerr was slain in front of the market cross, in 1624, by rough borderers who came to it armed with hagbuts and pistols. An excess of drink was usually the cause of fights and resulted in a busy day for the fair keepers or later the town guards and policemen.

> *A wee soup drink dis unco weel*
> *To had the heart aboon;*
> *It's gude as lang's a canny chiel*
> *Can stand steeve in his shoon.*
> *But gin a birkie's owr weel sair'd,*
> *It gars him often stammer*
> *To pleys that bring him to the guard,*
> *An' eke the Council-chawmir,*
> *Wi' shame that day.*
>
> *Hallow Fair,* Robert Fergusson, 1772

Fykes Fair

> *A singular fair, held annually at the Clauchan o' Auchencairn;*
> *it begins at ten o'clock at night, continuing to the morning,*
> *and through part of the next day. All the drinkers, floriers*
> [swaggerers], *cutty gliers* [short lassie fond of winking] *and*
> *curious folks, attend from all parts of Galloway; and when so*
> *many such characters are met, any one may conclude, what for*
> *a fair it is; that it is one of the most blackguard gatherings in*
> *the south of Scotland.*
>
> *The Scottish Gallovidian Encyclopedia,* John Mactaggart, 1824

Fairs attracted a varied section of the rural community. At Dumfries, Richard Franck, a traveller, gives this description of his impressions:

*In the midst of that town is their market place in the centre
of which stands their tolbooth, the mid-steeple, round about
which the rabble sit, that nauseate the very air with their
tainted breath, so perfumed with onions, that to an
Englishman it is almost infectious.*

Northern Memoirs, Richard Franck, 1656

and at Inverness,

You may see one [a Highlander] *eating a large onion without
salt or bread; another knawing on a carrot, etc. These are
rareties not to be had in their own parts of the country.*

Letters From the North, Captain Burt, 1735

Gypsies

At North Queensferry, bands of gypsies hired horses to ride to
the fair in the north of Scotland. The local boatmen considered
them to be friends and gave them the nickname of 'Killie
Wheesh' – the lads that take the purses. On completing the
crossing of the Forth the boatmen shook the hand of each
gypsy and wished him a 'good market'.

Pickpockets

In the midst of the crowds at a fair pockets were picked as if
by magic. The female gypsies wore rings which had concealed
pieces of sharpened steel incorporated inside them. These were
activated by a spring when a fist was made. The pressure
released a tiny knife which was used to slit the cloth of the
pocket. The dexterous hand could then remove the contents
which were speedily passed to an accomplice.

Taxes

Taxes were levied on every item sold at a fair, usually by
the local laird. In 1876 Sir George Elphinstone had a market on
ground at St Ninian's Croft at the Bridgend, Glasgow, in
opposition to the burgh market, for which he charged. Up until
1862 the Duke of Buccleuch, at St Boswell's, every July the
eighteenth, levied customs on every item brought to the market;
a half-pence for every three pounds of butter, a penny for every
web of cloth, fourpence for a load of oatmeal and twopence for
a puppet show.

If tenants took their goods or custom to a fair or market outwith the jurisdiction of the local laird, he often set up his own and compelled them to use it and pay the duty. Lord Maxwell set up such a fair at Milton of Urr, in Galloway, and forced tenants of the Stewartry of Kirkudbright to deal there. The town council of Dumfries took him to the Privy Council, in 1672, and won their case. Five years later they paid him one thousand merks Scots to close his market. In Kelso at the fair held on the Green on St James' Day, August the fifth, the magistrates were in attendance and split the profits between the town council and the local laird. There were a number of free fairs held in a year.

Location

Fairs took place in market squares, on nearby moors or mosses, along streets and on the links of coastal towns and in churchyards. In Keith there are five blind arches still visible on the east wall of the churchyard where merchants placed their stalls.

Fair trading

Fair trading was an essential of all transactions, no private dealing was officially permitted and every merchant had to be given a fair deal. This meant that they had to wait until a bell, often the Church bell, was rung before selling or buying could begin. At Dalkeith the selling did not begin until noon and occasionally in the town records there are complaints about 'selling before the bell' which was a fineable offence.

Fore-stalling

This meant deals which were set up by merchants giving them an unfair advantage. They were fined if caught in the act. To prevent this, in Brechin, the youngest baillie had to ride out with a guard to meet incomers about five miles outside of the town.

Smuggling

Another name for smuggling was 'fair trading'. In some areas many of the goods sold at the fairs had not paid honest taxes. Smuggling was a way of life in Galloway and along the coasts of Angus and the North-East. The Stoneykirk Fairs in Galloway were reputedly rife with goods which had not paid duty.

Morals

Fairs were considered by many people, especially the ministers of the Church of Scotland as places of over-indulgence, drunkenness and injurious to morals because the promiscuous dancing (which meant a man and a woman dancing together) often took place. They were 'nuisances which should be abolished', 'led to idleness and drunkenness', 'the pedlars wares threaten, by attracting young females to them, to do injury to their morals' according to comments made about local fairs in the *Second Statistical Account of Scotland*, 1835. However, at Ellon, Aberdeenshire the minister felt that such reports 'exaggerated the evils'.

Attractions

> *For months before frequent deposits were being made in our Penny Savings Bank, and when at last the anxiously expected morning arrived, with what feelings of pride did we make a 'run' upon the bank, riffling its coffers of the accumulated coppers, not satisfied until its whole contents were transferred to the pockets of our new moleskins, donned for the first time in honour of 'The Moss' – alas! for us, to be soon either unluckily spent at the Lucky Poke, lost at the Wheel of Fortune, covered from our view at the Dice or completely taken from us at the Rowley Powley [a game of skittles]. This fair is the principal one in the Vale, [of Leven] and district; for although those of Carman Sands and Bonhill and Drymen, are all important enough in their own way, none of them creates half the interest, or attracts anything like the number of visitors, as that at Balloch. It is, moreover, the only fair that is honoured by a total cessation of public work, and consequently the elite of the Vale is seen to considerable advantage on 'Moss Day'.*
>
> Epilogue to *The Old Vale and its Memories*,
> J. Ferguson and J.G. Temple, 1929

At most fairs there were booths for Punch and Judy; Aunt Sally – 'three balls a penny, every time you knock them down you get a coconut'; cup and ball; giants and giantesses, dwarfs, Ride Dick Turpin's Horse Black Bess, the excitement of this being in how quickly the man could turn the handle to try to throw the person off; Rowly-powley – a stick was thrown at pegs which had pieces of penny gingerbread on them. If you knocked it off you won, swings, round-a-bouts and many other favourites. There were also Penny Geggies or theatres, especially in the nineteenth century, which were theatrical shows.

Hear, hear! what a discordant din,
Wi' trumpets, cymbals, drums,
The warnin' cry o' 'Just begin,'
From every showman comes.
Haste, tumble in – no time to lose
Fun ridin' upon fun –
See an' believe, without excuse-
Such feats were never done
Before this day.
'There's Punch', an' cokalorum tricks
Ingenious machinery –
Dwarfs, giants, measurin' seven foot six –
The wild beasts menagerie.
The manly-lookin', oe'r grown child
A wonder of the age,
For strikin' features, visage mild,
The boast o' history's page.
In any day.

Humours of Glasgow Fair, Gabriel Neil, 1850

A description of a fair, at Tarbert, Argyll, in the form of fiction, paints the sights, sounds and atmosphere.

The square in front of the house was crammed with horses.
Strung around the harbour front were the booths, the shows,
the swings, the shooting-galleries, the ice-cream and fruit-stalls.
The nickering of mares, the clatter of hoofs, the cries of
showmen and jugglers; the yelling of coopers, negroes, and
men in charge of roulette-boards; the blasphemy of drunkards;
and over all the booming of the organ at the hobby horses.

Gillespie, J. MacDougall Hay, 1914

Dressing the cross

On fair days the young girls often rose early to dress the market cross with flowers. Another use made of the market cross was by illiterates who touched it as a seal of a bargain. Often, on the eve of the fair especially, the May hirings, the children decked with flowers would parade through the town, following a band.

> *Ra-ra-rae, the nicht afore the Fair!*
> *The drums in the walligate, the pipes i' the air.*
> *Silk an sateen.*
> *Gold an nankeen,*
> *Tig! for the morn's the Fair Day.*
>
> Traditional

Fairings

These were trinkets, little gifts, toys or sweets for the children, or ribbons, often bought by the young men for their sweethearts. Toys which were popular were rag dolls, wooden soldiers, mouth organs or 'moothies', as they were known, spinning tops – 'peeries', which had a groove for a leather lace or a piece of string to make them whirl; yo-yo's; peashooters and pocket knives.

Food and drink

The farmers who came in from the country paid their accounts quarterly. In *Gillespie*, Gillespie, the merchant, receives the farmers' payments and in return he feeds them dinner at his house.

> *The dinner dishes and cutlery were washed and set on the table, and part of the dinner prepared by the time that the organ of the hobby horses began to bray at nine o'clock. Gillespie always ordered a 'sheep's inside' for the occasion, Topsail [his servant] with hands smeared with blood, cleaned it out; carried the head and trotters to the blacksmith to be singed; made black puddings with blood supplied by the butcher. She served up the head and trotters with the black puddings and the liver. Gillespie saw it as the cheapest way to feed the farmers, who arrived in the afternoon with hunger in their big red faces.*
>
> Gillespie, J. MacDougall Hay, 1914

At Glasgow Fair cow heels and tripe were a favourite dish, as were boiled whelks, picked out with a pin. Bridies were enjoyed at Forfar and baps and butteries at Aberdeen.

Supply of liquor

The inns did a roaring trade in the town on fair day but many fairs were held outside an area where there were hostelries. Refreshment tents were put up and were a part of the scene at most fairs. An enterprising shepherd, who lived in a cottage on Carman Moor between Balloch and Cardross, applied for, and was granted, a licence to sell liquor at Carman Hill Fair and Cardross Fair. At the Carol Fair, held in November at Ruthven, some householders made a profit by supplying luncheons and selling liquor during the days of the fair. Brewster wives offered ale for sale at the Hallow Fair in Edinburgh's Castle Barns, near Fountainbridge.

Sweeties

These were popular with children and adults alike. There were no commercially manufactured sweets, they were all hand-made, often at the fair, especially puff candy and toffee balls. Lozenges and pink sweetie hearts which had messages of love printed on them sold well as did sticks of rock with the name of the town imprinted on every bite.

Different areas had their own speciality. Edinburgh rock was soft as was Strathaven toffee, more like a fudge; macaroon was made from potatoes; Hawick Balls; Berwick Cockles; Soor-plooms – originally from Galashiels, these were supposed to have first been made to commemorate the Braw lads o' Gala Water who had a skirmish with English raiders who were overcome while eating unripe plums.

Robert Coltart of Melrose became immortalized for his candy, which he sold at fairs around the borders, in the song 'Coulter's Candy'.

> *Ally Bally, Ally Bally bee,*
> *Sittin' on ma mammies knee*
> *Cryin' for a wee bawbee*
> *Tae buy some Coultar's candy.*
>   Traditional

Lunnan Candy

This was made and marketed for coughs and colds as well as coming recommended as a cure for shortness of breath.

Treats

Other popular treats were gingerbread often cut into fancy shapes, especially gingerbread men, for the children. Toffee apples were also great favourites as were cinnamon and liquorice sticks and sugarolly water. Raisins and oranges were considered an exciting rarity and if there was a 'pokey hat man' selling ice-cream from his barrow the day was made.

Accommodation

The surge of people converging on a small town caused problems of accommodation. Every inn or public house, every home, barn and kiln was filled to bursting point for miles around. Tents were often erected to house the visitors. 'Andrew Wilson's Tent' remained as a place name near Keith long after the fair had dwindled away. He put up his tent at the side of the road on the western slope of Balloch Hill and offered lodgings and refreshments at the time of the Summer Eve Fair.

FAIRS

Feeing fairs

All farm workers, whether leaving or staying on at term-time had a holiday on fair days.

Farm workers' wages were generally paid half-yearly at the Whitsun and Martinmas terms. This was when fairs were held to allow farm workers to move to a different farm. Farmers, and in bigger farms their grieves, would attend and sign up new workers with a handshake and a dram to seal the bargain. This was as binding a contract as any written one. They were said to be 'arled' and if they left before the full time agreed they lost their pay. Men were needed for all types of work – ploughing, sewing, harrowing, etc. Some were 'orra' men, who could turn their hands to any job, while others were experts with horses, especially Clydesdales, and knew that they could drive a hard bargain. Other feeing fairs were held around Candlemas for hinds and Lammas for shearers and reapers.

At Saltcoats 'such as those that come from the Highlands' were in demand at Candlemas while at Arderseir near Inverness, at Lammas, in August, female reapers from Ross and

Cromarty came to be hired carrying their plaids, cheese and fruit. Good workers could hold out for the highest bid. They gathered at the public houses after being fee'd to have a drink or three to celebrate. This was often followed by dancing to a fiddler until the wee sma' hours. At Perth, in August 1593, the Kirk Session complained about Highland reapers sauntering on the streets on Sunday waiting to be hired at the Monday market.

Muckle Friday

Feeing Day in Aberdeen was known as Muckle Friday and Ellon Fair, held at Marymas, August the fifteenth was one of the most important in the North-East until the coming of the railways.

Dairymaids

The female dairymaids and domestics were often hired by the farmer's wife at the fair. Many left school one day and went to be fee'd the next. They then had a great time flirting with the lads, dancing and enjoying the sideshows and went home to get ready to arrive at the farm on the agreed day. If anyone did not turn up on time they were sacked. They often started as kitchen maids and had a hard time learning the ropes.

> _'Mither, I'm gaun tae Lowden Fair,'_
> _'Lassie, what are ye gaun to do there?'_
> _'I'm gaun to buy ribbons, an' laces an' lawn_
> _To put on my head when I get a gudeman.'_
> _Vagabond Songs and Ballads_, Robert Ford, ed., 1904

Another young lady met on the road from Milngavie to Glasgow gains the shelter of an umbrella for the first time:

> _A friend and I struck frae Millguy;_
> _For Glasgow town we took our way;_
> _When all along the road was strung,_
> _With lads and bonnie lassies gay._
> _When drawing nigh, one I did spy,_
> _Was walking slowly by hersel';_
> _For fear the rain her dress might stain,_
> _I did display my umberell._

'Where are you gaun, my bonnie lass?
How far now are you gaun this way?'
'To Glasgow town, sir, I am bound,
For this, you know, is feeing-day.'
Says I, 'The day seems wet to be,
Although the morning did look fine.'
Smiling she said, 'I am afraid,
I'll no be in by feeing time.'

'Heeze up your heart, my bonnie lass,
We'll ha'e gude weather by an' by;
And don't be sad, when with a lad,
A roving baker frae Millguy.
And if you'll here accept my cheer,
A cup o' tea, or glass o' wine;
We'll rest a while, and yet we will
Reach Glasgow ere the feeing-time.'

She gave consent, and in we went
Into an ale-house by the way;
Wi' crack an' glass the time did pass
Till baith forgot the feeing-day.
The clock struck three, she smiled on me,
'Young man,' says she, 'the fault is thine;
The night is on, and I'm from home –
Besides I've lost the feeing-time.'

'My lass, don't grieve, for while I live,
I ne'er intend to harm you;
The marriage tie if you will try,
Your baker lad will aye prove true.'
'I am too young to wed a man –
My mother she has nane but me,
Yet I'll comply, and ne'er deny;
Far better wed than take a fee.'

We spent the night in merriment,
We wedded finely were next day;
And aye my lass she did confess
'Twas well to lose the feeing-day.'

My love and me, we sae agree,
I'm sure she never will repine;
But every day will smile and say,
'I'm glad I lost the feeing-time.'

Vagabond Songs and Ballads, Robert Ford, ed., 1904

Packin' Day

This was the name given to the day before the flitting (or moving) to another farm. If it was at a distance the carrier would often be hired to lift the kist and the meal bine (chest) to the new place while the farmworker would walk.

Besides the flitting of housewives, we had the servant lassies
from our parish farms shifting the boxes to their new places.
Dalmuir station was quite busy with the sonsy Jeannies on
Thursday who had their trunks with their braws piled high
up at the station.

Clydebank Press, 30th May 1896

Orra lads

There were also young lads who left home to work on the farm.

My mither was wae, for my father was deid,
And they'd threatened tae tak' the auld hoose ower oor heid;
Her earnings were sma', and the meal it grew dear;
I was auldest o' five, and could whiles see a tear.
As she cam hame at nicht, glistening bricht in her een –
Half hid, as if't didna want tae be seen.
I saidna' a word, but ma hert it wad ache,
An' a wished I wis big for ma puir mither's sake.

The farmers aroon wanted herds for their kye,
An' ma mither she said she had ane that wad try;
I trembled, I mind, half in fear, half in joy,
When a farmer ca'ed in jist tae look at the boy.
He bade me staun up, an' he thocht I wis wee
But ma frank honest face, he said, pleased his e'ee,
He wad tak me an' try me ae half year tae see,
For a pair o' new shoon an' a five-shillin' fee.

147

Oh! we were glad tae hear tell o't – a bargain wis struck,
An' he gied us a saxpence o' arles for gude luck,
Ma troosers an' jaiket were patched for the day,
An' ma mither convoyed me a lang mile o'way.
Wi' charges an' warnin's 'gainst a' sorts o' crime,
An' rules she laid doon, I thocht hard at the time.
Though the kye should rin wrang, I wis never to lee,
Though they sent me awa', withoot ma shoon or fee.

Sae I set tae ma wark and I pleased richt weel –
At a wave o' a haun I wis aff like an eel.
But ma troubles cam on for the fences were bad,
An' the midsummer flies gart the cattle rin mad;
Or the cauld blashy weather, sair drenched wi' the rain,
Till wee thochts o' leavin' wad steal through ma' brain;
But wi' courage I aye dashed the tear frae ma' e'e,
When I thocht on ma shoon an' ma five-shillin' fee.

Syne the lang-looked-for Martinmas cam wi' ma store,
And proudly I coonted it twenty times o'er;
Though years since are fled, in a fortunate train,
I never hiv felt sic a rapture again.
Not the sailor, when safe through the breakers has steered,
Nor Waterloo's victor when Blucher appeared,
E're felt what I felt, when I placed on the knee
O' a fond-herted mither my five-shillin' fee.

The Five-shillin' Fee, Anon. (but possibly John Campbell, 1850)

Cottars

These were the married men who generally were fee'd for twelvemonths from Whitsun Term to the following Whitsun. They were given tied cottages and their wives often worked in the dairy or did other work on the farm. In the 1920s, they could expect around £60 per year plus the house rent-free, four pints of milk per day, two loads of coal, a load of potatoes, a half boll of oatmeal and a load of dung. They could also grow vegetables, keep a hen or two and perhaps a pig.

Qualifications

There were from time to time complaints about a lack of references or qualifications but most farmers chose their workers by word of mouth recommendations. The farmers also passed on word to one another. 'How are the brose caups sellin' the day?' they would ask when they wanted to know the going rate for the ploughmen. The ploughmen enjoyed a good moan about their conditions.

> There's some that sing o' Comar Fair,
> An' sound out an alarm,
> But the best sang that e'er was sung,
> It was about the Term;
> The term-time is drawing near
> When we will a' win free,
> An' wi' the weary farmers
> Again we'll ne'er agree.
>
> Wi' broad-tail'd coats and quaker hats,
> And whips below their arms,
> They'll hawk and ca' the country round
> Until they a' get farms.
> Their boots a' glawr and glitterin'
> Wi' spurs upon their heels;
> Yet though they ca' the country round
> Ye winna find sic deils.
>
> They'll tip ye on the shoulder
> And speir gin ye're to fee;
> They'll tell ye a fine story
> That's every words a lee;
> They'll tell ye a fine story,
> And get ye tae perform;
> But, lads, when ye are under them
> Ye'll stand the raging storm.
>
> They'll tak' ye tae an ale-hoose
> An' gie ye some sma' beer;
> They'll tak a drap unto themsel's
> Till they get better cheer;

And when the bargain's ended
They'll toll ye oot a shillin',
And grunt and say the siller's scarce –
The set o' leein' villains!

On cauld kail and tawties
They'll feed ye up like pigs,
While they sit at their tea and toast,
Or ride into their gigs.
The mistress must get, 'Mem' – and ye
Maun lift yer cap tae her;
And ere ye find an entrance
The master must get, 'Sir.'

The harvest time, when it comes on
They'll grudge ye Sabbath rest;
They'll let ye tae the worship,
But they like the workin' best.
The diet hour it vexes them,
And then to us they'll say –
'Come on my lads, ye'll get yer rest
When lyin' in the clay.'

They'll say unto the foreman,
'Keep on when leading grain,
And dinna let the orra lads
Stand idle at the end;
I pay tham a' good wages,
And pray ye tae get on;
For when they're dead and in the grave
Their's mair when they are done.'

Vagabond Songs and Ballads, Robert Ford, ed., 1904

Having another worker who already knew the grieve of a farm was also a good way for the man waiting to be fee'd to get 'set on'.

As I went down to Ellon Fair
Aince on a day to fee,
Likewise an opportunity
My comrades for to see.

150

And steerin' thro' the market
An auld neebor chanced to see;
And when I stepped up to him
He asked was I to fee.
He told me he was leevin',
Likewise his neebor tee;
He said the grieve did want a hand,
And he thocht that I wid dee.

He stept up unto the grieve,
Says, 'Here's a man to fee,
I think he'll suit you very weel,
If wi' him ye can agree.'

He told to me some of the work
That I would have to do;
He said I would have little else
But cart and hold the ploo.
He asked at me my wages,
What they were gaun to be;
So in a short time after
Wi' him I did agree.

Traditional

When they went to the fair the lads would wear a spear of corn in their bonnet or the lapel of their jacket to show that they were available for hire and remove it once they had a position.

Testimonials
The kirk session of the parish to which the farmworker was moving demanded that the farmer obtain a testimonial from the worker giving details of their moral state from the kirk session of the parish where they had previously attended the church.

Marriage
Many men met their future wives at the fairtime. In some places it was said that a good harvest ensured a rash of weddings at Martinmas. Many couples, after a year of handfasting, took advantage of the attendance of a priest at a fair to make the marriage legal.

FAIRS FOR SPECIFIC PRODUCTS

Seed fairs

In spring many towns and villages held Seed fairs. Flax was a useful commodity grown throughout the lowlands as was lint, other forms of seed, including seed potatoes were also available at the right season. Seed corn and kale plants were sold at Lauder, Biggar and at Stoneykirk Shore Fair; at Dalkeith, oats were sold; at Haddington; wheat while Edinburgh had its Grass Market where grain was sold.

Links Market

Linkstown was a village in Fife. It had one street about three-quartes of a mile long and was a burgh of regality, which gave it the right to appoint burgesses and hold two fairs annually. Through time Linkstown joined up with Abbotshall to form the larger burgh of Kirkcaldy. The April fair was mainly for lintseed and linen goods. This gradually fell away but the Links Market, as a carnival, still takes place along the promenade.

Lintseed Saturdays

These took place in Kirkintilloch, on several Saturdays in the spring. They were held at Eastside which was left wide for that purpose. Barter was often the way of paying for goods and little money changed hands. The farmers arrived with their horses laden with lint carried in panniers. These horses were lined up along both sides of Eastside and down the Ledgate.

> Lintseed Saturdays were at one period [in the 1840 s] great occasions for the sale of this commodity, and flax markets were previous to this also of no little importance – the buyers and sellers coming to Eastside from as far north as Fintry; Kirkintilloch fairs had not then fallen on degenerate days and were held on the second Tuesday of May, last Thursday of July and the twenty-first of October. The May and October fairs are still observed, but their ancient glory has departed. Shows, merry-go-rounds and similar enticements are now the chief features on fair day, for no one now thinks of going there to buy merchandise, or of taking to it either cattle or produce for sale.
> The History of Kirkintilloch, John Horne, 1910

Edinburgh had its Lawn Market. Ladykirk, Dysart, Inverness and Lockerbie held markets, while at Aberdeen at Eastertime,

There was some gay wark, at the Muckle Paise Market,
Where wives bought their linen an' sheets in the spring.

Rhymes, W. Anderson, 1851

Wool

Many fairs were held to sell wool and cloth. Both English and Scottish dealers would be present. At Saltcoats boats from the Isle of Arran would arrive the night before and a fair for wool also took place at Brodick, Inverness and Rink, near Jedburgh. Hoddan, near Lockerbie, gave its name to a coarse black and white woollen cloth, hodden grey, popular for everyday garments throughout Scotland. A dandling rhyme used for balancing a child across the knee and jumping them up and down like a horse ride, gives Berwick as a fair for wool.

Ride a mile tae Berwick toon
Tae buy a pun o' 'oo.

Traditional

Sooty Poke Fair

This fair was held annually close to the old church of Kirkmadrine in Galloway. Its unusual name came from the weavers from Stoneykirk bringing their webs of cloth, which had been woven during the winter, for sale. These they carried in bags saturated with soot from the smoke from their fires.

Cloths, tartans, plaiding and blankets were also favourite items to be found at many fairs. At Glenorchy, at St Conan's Fair, craft competitions were held. At Shotts a yarn fair was held in August up until the early part of the nineteenth century. Home-spun cloth and yarn were sold. A balance for weighing the material hung at the Tron Knowe.

Implements

Some fairs specialized in the sale of implements both domestic, agricultural or commercial. The Old Cumnock Scythe Fair was widely known and special sand from Loch Doon was sold for sharpening the blade. At Leith merchants from abroad arrived with timber and local merchants sold farm carts, implements and machinery.

> *'Mither, I'm gaun to Lowden Fair,'*
> *'Laddie, what are ye gaun to do there?'*
> *'I'm gaun tae buy horses, harrows, and plows,*
> *An' start wi' a pair on Glowerowerem Knowes.'*
>
> Vagabond Songs and Ballads, Robert Ford, ed., 1904

Clatt Fair

At St Mallock's Fair held at Clatt for eight days in June, Highlanders brought wrought iron girds which they had made and exchanged them for wine with merchants from the Lowlands. The pipers passed around their hats for contributions.

At Kilbirnie on St Brinan's Day, in May, kitchen and dairy utensils, spinning wheels and reels, roasting-jacks and toasting forks and cooper's barrels were popular. At Glasgow, masons and builders traded stones, bricks and pavement slabs at the top of Stockwell Street in the eighteenth century.

At St Conan's Fair, Glenorchy merchants arrived from Doune, Callender, Perth and Stirling with knives, pistols, and swords carried in panniers across the backs of their horses.

LIVESTOCK

Other fairs and markets were held at which certain types of animals or even breeds were to the fore. Ellon Fair near Aberdeen was important for cattle until the coming of the railways which made the markets of the south much easier to reach. Sheep were brought from Ross and Cromarty and Sutherland, ponies from Shetland and cattle from the Western Isles. Pigs were also sold. The sale of hides to tanners played a large part in the local economy.

Cattle

The Union of the Crowns, in 1603, boosted the Highland cattle industry. Sometimes the cattle were made to swim across a minch to a local fair, perhaps at Beauly or Muir of Ord where they were bought and then driven on to one of the Trysts. In the eighteenth and nineteenth centuries cattle bought in Galloway were collected in droves and driven to Norwich for sale. These were known as St Faith's Cattle.

Trysts
In the eighteenth century Crieff Tryst, especially in the autumn, was important for the sale of cattle as English drovers came prepared to spend large amounts of money. In 1777 the main Trysts were moved to Falkirk and by the mid-nineteenth century around 150,000 cattle were sold there in the autumn. Others were held at Pennymuir, Brechin, Oxnam and Hounam. Gifford and Edinburgh's Gorgie Market were fairs not fixed by statute or charter, but were meeting places for owners of thousands of livestock from all parts of the country up until the mid-nineteenth century.

Patie's penny
This was a tax levied up to the eighteenth century on cattle slaughtered at Perth. Originally it was a tax in the Middle Ages for the upkeep of the wax candles burned at the altar of St Peter in the old church.

Horses
At Brodick, Isle of Arran, farmers bought young horses which arrived from the Western Isles. These were usually already broken-in for ploughing and carting. Steamers brought folk from the mainland for a day's enjoyment. In October a further sale, usually for foals, was held.

Keltonhill Fair
This was the gathering place for the gypsies of Galloway and it was held at Rhonehouse on the Fair Green on St John's Day. Billy Marshall, the famous gypsy king, never missed this fair. It was a well known horse market and was moved to the market Hill at Castle Douglas in 1860.

> *Sae here's to the glens growing thickly wi' hazels*
> *An' here's to days I will never see mair;*
> *An' here's tae the tinkers, wallets and cuddies,*
> *Whilk dadjell ilk years tae braw Keltonhill Fair.*
> Keltonhill Fair, *Scottish Gallovidian Encylopedia*, John Mactaggart, 1824

Pork

In Dumfermline, in November and December, Puddin' Fairs were held for the sale of pork. Pigs were slaughtered at the oncoming of winter and white and mealy puddings were made.

> *It fell aboot the Martinmas time*
> *An' a gay time it was then o!*
> *When oor guid wife had puddins to mak*
> *An' she baked them in the pan o!*
>
> Traditional

Hares

At Dumfries a fair held at the Whitesands annually sold thirty thousand hare-skins.

Lambs

Lambs were sold at several fairs – Ettrick, Stirling, Luss and Langholm, which took place on July the twenty-sixth, the day before the Common Riding. The Lockerbie Lammas Fair was the largest and that at Auchinleck the latest held in Scotland.

Whelks

Cardross 'Wulk' Fair was held on the shores of the Firth of Clyde. People travelled for miles around to visit it, many walking across the Carman Hill from the Vale of Leven.

> *As there was no Clyde Purification Scheme in operation in*
> *those days, it was marvellous illness did not follow the picking*
> *with a preen [pin] the boiled whelks taken from Cardross*
> *Shore. Cardross Fair was associated with wading, inhaling*
> *the smell of the alleged sea, the eating of gingerbread cut from*
> *blocks like bars of soap, the selecting and sucking pink-coloured*
> *and rose-flavoured sweetie hearts the size and weight of a*
> *girl's peever [hop-scotch stone]. To those unable to afford*
> *the price of the train, it was a toilsome tramp home over the*
> *Carman Hill.*
>
> Epilogue to The Old Vale and its Memories,
> J. Ferguson and J. G. Temple, 1929

In 1900, this was a favourite outing for Clydebank people who went by train to Cardross Whelk Fair.

Summer Fairs
Glasgow Fair

Established by a charter from William the Lion in 1190, this fair was originally held at the rock in the garden of Greyfriars Monastery, near what is now Albion Street. It was called the Craignaught and was where the magistrates made their announcements. Later it moved to the Stockwell-gait which was the main entrance to the city from the south where it was described in unflattering terms:

> *It was interrupted on the Wednesday of the annual fair with an endless barrier of restive horses and neighing stallions; while, on the Friday, it for ages displayed, amid the lowing of bulls and bestial, the coarse courting of country cubs, and the unsophisticated merry-making of whisky inspired ploughmen and laughing cherry-cheeked dairy-maids.*
>
> *The Stockwell was at that time, likewise, the rendezvous of all country servants open for hire, as well as those from the city, who were usually arled at the Brigend ... The freaks of Punch and Judy, and the elegancies of ground and lofty tumbling were then displayed at the north end of the Old Bridge, or in the houses and closes at the south end of the street ... [It] could always boast of at least a dozen painted Jezebels, who in front of several booths outraged Terpsichore as much in their movements as the Dutch concert of hurdie-gurdies and fiddles, which guided their heavy fantastic toes, set defiance to both time and tune.*
>
> Glasgow and Its Clubs, John Strang, 1894

At one time vast spectacular visual panoramics were on display, each year's trying to outdo the one before. These included waterfalls and re-enactments of the battles of the Boer War. The Fair was always popular, but it gradually deteriorated into a showmen's carnival held first at Vinegar Hill and latterly on the Glasgow Green.

Rothesay Fair

> *This was held on two days in the middle of July but has degenerated into a series of stalls of games of chance and*

*perhaps skill, of palmistry tents, and of auctions, while a
hand-turned hobby-horse takes the place of the magnificent
steam merry-go-round with its whirling steeds, the braying
organ with its dance tunes, and the gorgeous decorations all
so dear to the heart of a child.*

Third Statistical Account, The County of Bute, 1956

Fair of the Female Saints

On the Isle of Loch Tay there stood a priory. In 1122, King
Alexander I granted a Charter to the monks of Scone Abbey
in memory of his Queen, Sybilla, who died on the island and
was buried there. It became a nunnery. Every year on the
twenty-sixth of July the sisters attended a fair at Kenmore. It
was known as the Fair of the Female Saints. There they sold
their work to make money to maintain their priory and offered
help to the poor and infirm.

Lammas fairs

A number of Lammas fairs or markets were held throughout
the country but probably the most famous is that at St Andrews
which is still held in the streets, although in a changed form.

*Yesterday the showmen from all over the country arrived in the
town for the annual Lammas Market and set up their stalls and
round-a-bouts on the cobbled part of the street.*

The Scotsman, 8th August 1959

It was established by Charter from James VI, in 1620, and was
originally a feeing fair. In 1832 the Magistrates of St Andrews
took drastic action to try to prevent the spread of cholera, which
at that time was rife.

*The Magistrates of St Andrews hereby give public intimation,
that in consequence of the alarming increase of cholera
throughout the country, they have resolved to prohibit all
persons coming from infected districts selling goods, wares or
merchandise of any kind, in the ensuing Lammas market.*

The Fife Herald, 19th July 1832

In Orkney the Lammas Fair was held on the first Tuesday after
the eleventh of August in Kirkwall and was a well attended

occasion. Carnwath, Paisley, Keith, Melrose, Tarland, Hoddam and many other towns and villages also held Lammas Fairs.

Summer Eves Fair

This fair was held on the first Tuesday of September at Keith in Banffshire. The name is a corruption of the local titular saint, St Maelrubha or Maree, as he was known.

> *To it the whole merchants of Aberdeen, leaving their shops almost empty, with all their goods repaired [came to], and very little unsold was carried back. They were transported on horseback, in packs of sacking, each one making one load . . . All of the carriers, and many of the smaller farmers in the vicinity of Aberdeen, were employed for ten or twelve days before the market; they travelled in caravans, from a dozen to forty together; their approach was announced with joy, when first descried upon the brow of the distant hill . . . Numbers of trading people, and foremost manufacturers from Glasgow, Perth and Dundee, and from other towns in the south, were met by all the merchants in the western Highlands and northerly parts of the kingdom, from the distance even of Kirkwall, in the Orkney Isles, for settling accompts [sic] and arranging new commissions. To this fair also was brought the whole manufacture of coarse woollen cloths, with all the black cattle and horses, it is still much the greatest fair in the north.*
> The Book of the Chronicles of Keith, Rev. Garden, 1880

Hallowmas

Hallow fairs were held in the autumn in a number of places. The most famous was that held in Edinburgh and described by Robert Fergusson in his poem, the 'Hallow Fair', written in 1772.

> *At Hallowmas, whan nights grow lang,*
> *And starnies shine fu' clear,*
> *Whan folk, the nippin cald to bang*
> *Their winter hap-warms wear.*
> *Near Edinbrough a fair there had,*
> *I wat there's nane whase name is,*
> *For strappin dames and sturdy lads,*

And cap and stoup, mair famous
Than it that day.

Recruitment

At these gatherings all over the country recruitment sergeants were in attendance to persuade young men to join the army or navy and accept the King's Shilling.

> *The dinlin drums alarm our ears,*
> *The sergeant screechs fu' loud,*
> *'A' gentlemen and volunteers*
> *That wish your country gude*
> *Come here to me, and I sall gie*
> *Twa guineas and a crown,*
> *A bowl o' punch, that like the sea*
> *Will soum a lang dragoon*
> *Wi' ease this day.'*
>
> Hallow Fair, Robert Fergusson, 1772

Holy Fairs

The Holy Fairs which Robert Burns wrote about were not intentionally fairs but Sacramental Fast Days, days on which the Communion services of the Church of Scotland were held. These were usually in the spring and autumn. They were declared as fast days and no work was undertaken. Preparatory services were held on the previous Thursday and it is from these that the towns in Scotland derive their spring and autumn holiday weekends which differ throughout the country and are not, as in England, bank holidays. Thanksgiving services were held on the following Monday. However they often did turn into an excuse for fun and frolic and booths and tents were often put up to serve refreshments.

> *What must the consequences be when a whole countryside is*
> *thrown loose, and young lads and girls go home together by night*
> *in the gayest time of the year. When I was an apprentice I was*
> *a great frequenter of those occasions, and I know them so well*
> *that I would not choose a wife that had frequented them, or*
> *trust a daughter too much amongst these rambling saints.*
>
> First Statistical Account of Scotland, the Parish of Glassford, 1796

Mauchline

The Holy Communion described in Burns' poem took place on the second Sunday in August 1785. The open-air field Sacrament attracted the Weavers from Kilmarnock and other blackguards from miles around, according to Dr Edgar who wrote of it in *Old Church Life in Scotland* in 1790. There was always a problem of feeding and accommodating the vast numbers who attended. At Cambuslang in August 1743 it was estimated that three thousand participated and thirty thousand people attended. This led to the Communion only being held spasmodically in each Parish and sometimes it would be two years before another was held in the same area.

Robert Burns gives a vivid description of the scene as several ministers delivered sermons, each after his own style. The congregation are depicted as often being more interested in matters less than spiritual.

> *Here some are thinkin on their sins,*
> *An' some upo' their claes;*
> *Ane curses feet that fyl'd his shins*
> *Anither sighs an' prays:*
> *On this hand sits a chosen swatch,*
> *Wi' screw'd-up, grace-proud faces;*
> *On that, a set o' Chaps, at watch,*
> *Thrang winkin' on the lasses*
> *To chairs that day.*
>
> The Holy Fair, Robert Burns, 1786

Edinburgh

> *A great convention was held of the adherents to the seceding ministers of the Church of Scotland, in a square plain on the Braid Hills, two miles south of this city . . . There were about 5000 hearers at each sermon. (I mean of the household of faith), some of whom from South Britain and Ireland, besides the ungodly audience, consisting of many thousands, some of whom set fire to furze; others hunted the hare around them to create a disturbance, a certain huntsman having laid a plot to carry off the collection.*
>
> Caledonian Mercury, 22nd March 1738

Sunday markets

These markets were held by Charter from the king up until 1593 when the Earl of Wigton introduced a new Charter which conferred other privileges and led to the demise of the Sunday market. This Charter permitted all burghs of barony the right to hold a weekly market on the last day of every week and to have the privilege of holding two free fairs annually, which meant that taxes need not be paid by the merchants, on their goods.

> *A great number of drapers, fleshers and merchants, accused of keeping the market of Crail on the Sabbath [were] prohibited from repeating the offence under pain of exclusion – debarring their wives, bairns and servants from all benefit of the Kirk in time coming.*
>
> Parish of Crail, Kirk Session Records , 18th April 1582

However the Kirk Session discovered that it could not interfere with a Charter which was granted by King Robert the Bruce to Crail to hold a Sunday market in perpituity.

Glasgow

The date of the Glasgow Fair, July the seventh, occasionally fell on a Sunday and no market was held under penalty of a fine.

Fairs of all kinds declined in importance after the Industrial Revolution took hold and more people began to live in towns where entertainment was more regular and shops were open up to seventy hours per week. The name became associated with round-a-bouts and swings, the big wheel and roller-coasters which showmen who travel from town to town, as the pedlars did long ago, bring along and set up on the traditional fair area.

Agricultural shows

Most areas of Scotland hold an annual agricultural show. These are run by Agricultural Societies both big and small. They have taken over from fairs in many cases as meeting places for farmers. Their main purpose is the judging of livestock but there is usually horse-jumping, dog showing, machinery and crafts display as well as competitions for sheep shearing. There is a great variety of stalls which grow in number every year.

FOYS

These were farewell feasts or entertainments held for various occasions. They could be for someone departing for abroad, for changing their job or as a celebration of the end of a working season. They were often organized by an employer or by fellow workers.

Farewells
Western Isles

When someone was leaving home the neighbours gathered there to wish the voyager health and prosperity. They prayed for peace in the adopted land and sang a hymn of farewell. Gifts of hand-knitted stockings, gloves, plaids or a bonnet were made.

Bonello

This was a Galloway name for a parting feast. The occasion was merry until near the end when a sadness descended.

> *Kirrcormock's blyth lairdy, or he gaed awa'*
> *To fight and to florrie, through wide India,*
> *Invited his neebours about ane an a',*
> *To gie him a merry bonello . . .*
>
> *For sic an a shine, was seldom ere seen,*
> *Auld Scotland did vow she had ne'er wi' her een*
> *Beheld ought to match'd since the 'Kirk on the Green,'*
> *T' was a noble conducted bonello . . .*
>
> *In jugs and decanters, and noggins and kits,*
> *The drink it did circle, and mirth took her fits;*
> *Nae glumfie chiel sat, wi' his sneers and his skits,*
> *Scrutinising the famous bonello . . .*
>
> *Thus wi' dancing and drinking, the night slided by,*
> *Till Sol, wi' his gowd gift the Eastlin' sky,*
> *And mony a drunken chiel ouzily did ly,*
> *A bumpling wi' the bonello.*
>
> *Kirrcormock himsell was as fou as a witch,*
> *He danced till his lisk was beset wi' a stitch,*

For a' while his shanks after him he cud hitch,
He'd keep up his glorious bonello.

The Scottish Gallovidian Encyclopedia,
John Mactaggart, 1824

Anster Fair

The fair held at Anstruther was a farewell foy for those men and women who left to go to Great Yarmouth to work at gutting and packing the herring.

Feeing foys
Martinmas

This was a popular time for men and women who worked as farm servants to move to a new place. To mark the occasion a supper was put on by his or her fellow workers who were staying on at the farm for a futher term. Another foy was held to welcome the new workers a few days after their arrival.

Fishermen
Johnsmas Foy

There was a celebration called the Johnsmas Foy held, in June, at Lerwick which coincided with the arrival of the Dutch herring fleet.

Greenlanders

The Greenlandman's foy was a great institution, and generally took the form of a farewell supper and dance, and what may be called a good drink, a day or two before the ships sailed.

Fraserburgh, J. Canna, 1914

Lammas Foy

The Lammas Drave was the summer herring fishing and before the boats departed a feast was held in many ports.

Simmermil Foy

This was held in Shetland where a cruzie of fish-oil was lit and placed on the Johnsmas fire which burned outside their individual houses. It had to burn out completely to bring good fortune to the fishing. There were riddles and feasting and blessings were said.

Games and Gatherings

TOURNAMENTS

*T*he wappinshaw was a periodical muster of the irregular armed force of the country; it got its name from the more immediate purpose of the assembly – namely the exhibition of weapons and was held by districts or overlords. At these events it became popular to test the skills of the men in archery, rifle shooting and lancing as well as their skill on horseback and fleetness of foot. In many ways they were similar to the medieval tournaments. Reviews of troops sometimes took place on fair or feast days.

> *At fairs he play'd before the Spear-men,*
> *All gaily graithed in their gear-men:*
> *Steel bonnets, jacks, and swords so clear then,*
> *Like any bead.*
> *Now wha will play before such weir-men,*
> *Sen Habbie's dead.*

The Life and Death of the Piper of Kilbarchan, Sir Robert Sempill ofBeltrees, from *Poems of the Sempills of Beltrees*, James Patterson, 1849

Eglinton Tournament

In August 1839 at Eglinton Castle, near Irvine, the Earl of Eglinton held a spectacular pageant known as the Eglinton Tournament. Prince Louis Napoleon took part and a grand-daughter of the poet Richard Brinsley Sheridan – Lady Seymour, was the Queen of Beauty.

> *In August 1839 Irvine was temporarily crowded with strangers pouring in from sea and highway to witness the feats of the Eglinton Tournament.*
>
> Ordnance Gazetteer of Scotland, F. H. Groome, 1883

Wappinshaws

Non-attendance at these events was punishable by a fine.

> *In October 1575, Johne Wilsoune and James Andersoun, fleschouris, burgessis of Glasgow, ar fund in americiamentis and unlawis* [have a fine inflicted upon them] *for abseyntyng thame fra the generall wapynschawing haldin on Glasgow Greyne, the x day of October instant, thai being within the toun the said daye.*
>
> The History of Glasgow, George MacGregor, 1881

Edinburgh

At Edinburgh on New Year's Day a wappinshaw was held in the fifteenth century at which sword-fights, archery, ball-games and foot-races were included and the prizes were cheese and hams. Other sports were also included at wappinshaws such as football, shinty, horse-races jumping, putting the shot and quoiting. Occasions such as the Riding of the Marches and the Robin Hood games were also opportunities for enjoying these sports.

Stirling

At Stirling, in the sixtenth century, three flags were carried at the wappinshaw. The king's ensign was carried by someone representing the Provost and Baillies. The merchant's ensign and the craft's ensign were carried by members of those incorporated bodies. They marched through the town with the guilds parading behind their banner.

Dunfermline

In 1624 at a wappinshaw held at Dunfermline William Anderson, the son of John Anderson, bailiff of Dunfermline, and Charles Richeson, his servant,were shooting with some of their friends when a piece of shot landed in the thatch of a nearby house. It was a windy day and the fire spread from house to house until every house was on fire. The Abbey and the Church and a few slated houses were the only buildings to escape. The fire began at noon and was still burning at four o'clock. 'Goods, geir within houses, malt and victuals in kilns and barns, were consumed.' The town at that time had one hundred and twenty houses containing two hundred and eighty-seven families. A collection was taken in parish churches throughout Scotland for the victims and King Charles I ordered £500 sterling to be given for the relief of the poor. Some people believed it to be the will of God or else witchcraft rather than an accident.

Feast days and fairs

In some towns these sports, often run under the auspices of the incorporated trades, were transferred, originally, to the Feast day of the local titular saint, then later to the fair days.

> *Every burgh of Scotland of the least note, but more especially the considerable towns had their solemn play, or festival, when feats of archery were exhibited, and prizes distributed to those who excelled in wrestling, hurling the bar and other gymnastic exercises of the period. The usual prize for wrestling was a ram and a ring.*
>
> The Poetical Works, Walter Scott, 1897

However by the nineteenth century with the growth of towns after the Industrial Revolution they began to separate and develop into activities which took place in designated places. Racecourses were set up in Hamilton, Perth, Lanark and Ayr and Kelso; Athletic sports were run under the auspices of the police associations, football clubs and individual firms and became well attended communal events which raised money for charity. Another aspect of this was the incorporation of some of these activities in the Highland Games which, although their origins were much older, became popular, in their modern form, in the nineteenth century.

COMPETITIONS

Shooting
Siller arrows and siller guns

In many areas the winner was presented with a silver arrow for excellence at archery. Regular rifle shooting competitions were also held, the prize being a replica gun cast in silver. Several towns have these 'siller guns' and 'siller arrows' in their museums.

Guid Nychburris Festival

The Seven Trades of Dumfries received their 'siller gun' from King James V1 in the sixteenth century. It is competed for annually, in June, at the Guid Nychburris Festival and the winner is chaired along the Whitesands where the Provost presents him with a replica.

> *There is a small silver toy at Dumfries, in the form of a fusee or musket . . . carried by the trades in procession to a shooting-field near the town, whence the vicar used to bring it back home stuck in his hat.*
> Domestic Annals of Scotland, Vol 1, From the Revolution to the Rebellion 1745,
> Robert Chambers, 1874

Handsel Monday

There were shooting matches held at Stirling on Handsel Monday, the first monday after New Year, at which John Ferguson, otherwise known as Heather Jock, regularly carried away the prize. He was later charged with stealing cows and black cattle at a court in Stirling in 1812 and was deported. This was a popular day for shooting matches as it was a general holiday.

Popinjay

> *When the musters had been made, and duly reported, the young men, as was usual, were to mix in various sports, the chief of which was to shoot at the Popinjay, an ancient game formerly practised with archery but at this period with firearms. This*

was the figure of a bird, decked with party-coloured feathers,
as to resemble a popinjay or parrot. It was suspended from a
pole, and served as a mark, at which the competitors discharged
their fusees and carabines in rotation, at the distance of sixty
or seventy paces. He whose ball brought down the mark, held
the proud title of Captain of the Popinjay.

Old Mortality, Walter Scott, 1816

Kilwinning

Shooting is practised for prizes at the butts, point-blank
distance, about 26 yards. The prize, in this case, is some useful
or ornamental piece of plate [silver], given annually to the
company by the senior surviving archer.

Ordnance Gazetteer of Scotland, F.H. Groome, 1884

Archery

Originally a necessity in times of attack or even war, a good eye
for drawing a bow and shooting at a target developed into a
sport. The target was not, as in more recent times, a coloured
circle, but a representation in wood of a parrot usually called a
papingo. This was mounted on a pole and the archers had to
knock it down.

The people upon the Sabbath evenings, exercised themselves
with their bows and arrows, according to the ancient Scottish
laws for that purpose.

Parish of Callander, Statistical Account of Scotland, 1796

Royal Company of Archers

This exclusive Company was inaugurated under the Privy
Council of 1676 and Chartered by Queen Anne in 1704. In
1822 King George IV created them as King's Bodyguard in
Scotland. The Company consists of five hundred gentlemen led
by a Scots peer who is designated as Captain General. It is
nowadays purely a ceremonial body but membership holds
great prestige. They accompany the Queen on her visits to
Edinburgh. They still wear the traditional costume.

His dress and arms were splendid. He wore his national bonnet,
crested with a tuft of feathers, and with a Virgin Mary of
massive silver for a brooch . . . The Archer's gorget, arm-pieces,

169

*and gauntlets, were of the finest steel, curiously inlaid with
silver, and his hauberk, or shirt of mail, was as clear and
bright as the frostwork of a winter morning upon fern or briar.
He wore a loose surcoat, or cassock, of rich blue velvet, open at
the sides like that of a herald, with a large white St Andrew's
cross of embroidered silver bisecting both before and behind.
His knees and legs were protected by hose of mail and shoes of
steel. A broad strong poniard (called the Mercy of God) hung
by his right side – the baldric for his two-handed sword, richly
embroidered, hung upon his shoulder, but for convenience, he
at present carried in his hand that unwieldy weapon which the
rules of his service forbade him to lay aside.*

Quentin Durward, Walter Scott,1823

At one time the Royal Company of Archers held their
competitions at the Meadows in Edinburgh, wearing a special
shooting dress. In the nineteenth century these competitions
were transferred to the Butts.

Musselburgh
Since 1676 members of the Royal Company of Archers
competed for the Musselburgh Silver Arrow on the Links. The
winner took part in the March Riding which was held every
twenty-one years.

Kilwinning
A Company of Archers is recorded in Kilwinning in 1488.
Originally formed under royal authority, they later came under
the monks of Kilwinning Abbey. In July every year they shot
at a wooden figure of a parrot, called a papingo or popinjay,
which was suspended from a string to the top of a pole on the
120 foot high steeple of the church. Later it was made of
feathers and looked like a parrot. The archer who shot down the
popinjay was given the title of Captain of the Popinjay. It was
his place to act as master of ceremonies in the following year
and he had to host a ball and supper for the ladies of the town.
This festival was revived in 1952.

Ayr
In the nineteenth century at Ayr the Captain added his colours
to those already on the papingo which was then carried through

the town to be attached to the town steeple from where it had to be knocked down; the winner became the captain for the next year. A similar competition was held at Maybole.

In the sixteenth century students at the University of St Andrews were encouraged to practise archery by entering competitions.

Tilting at the ring

This was a popular sport in the Middle Ages. As part of their training knights practised jousting. For achieving accuracy a ring was hung at a practical height and the knight attempted, while on horseback, to catch it on the tip of his lance. This became a sport known as tilting at the ring. At Carnwath the Lady of Lee presented a gold ring to the winner. King James I granted the merchants of Stirling the right to tilt at the ring and at Dunkeld, King James V did likewise for the Society of Carters. The Bonny Earl of Moray, George Campbell, is described in the Ballad as an experienced knight dressed for war, 'He was a braw gallant and he rid at the ring'. Knights had to be of a certain standard before they could compete in such a tournament. It was a favourite sport at wappinshaws.

Picking up the Glove

This is a similar excercise where the rider has to pick up a glove from the ground on the point of his lance, while remaining in the saddle. This was a sport favoured by the Earl of Moray –

'He was a braw gallant and he played at the glove.'
        The Bonnie Earl of Moray, Traditional

Throwing the javelin

This is mentioned as a sport of the young aristocrats in the sixteenth century in many historical texts. In 1574 David Home of Wedderburn was considered an expert in several of these field sports.

Foot races

These were always popular and were the only form of athletic meeting of their time. It was not until the twentieth century that athletics meetings began to be held. Cross-country races, paper-chases and hound trailing were introduced and eventually towns and cities supported marathon and half-marathon races which were run through the streets and parks.

Braemar

A prize of a claymore and a purse of gold was decreed by King Malcolm, Ceann Mor, in the twelfth century, for a race to the top of Craig Choinnich. This was not an entirely altruistic gesture as the King required men who were fleet of foot as messengers and he wished to assess their abilities. The King, whose castle was at Kildrochit, and his retinue, assembled on the flat ground between the base of the hill and the River Dee to watch the race. Tradition has it that three brothers, the sons of McGregor of Ballochbuie, raced against each other and that the youngest, who started late, overtook the other two and reached the top in three minutes to win the prize. This feat was considered to be the origin of the Braemar Highland Gathering.

Galloway

Barons and lords employed men who were good runners as messengers, there being few good roads and no post offices until the late eighteenth century, and these limited to one each in Edinburgh and Glasgow. A servant of Lord Kenmure was renowned, at the many foot-races held in Galloway, for always coming in first. One night before the New Galloway Fair his Lordship decided to send this fellow on an errand to Edinburgh to give the other runners a chance. He ran there and back, a distance of 180 miles, in twenty-four hours and returned just in time to compete and win the race.

Red Hose Race

This was held at Carnwath on the day after the Lammas Lamb Fair in August. The pair of red hose were gifted by the Lockhart family of Lee and were much sought after. It was a steeplechase which involved cross-country running. In addition there were prizes for leaping, throwing the hammer, putting the stone and playing quoits. Originally the Red Hose were part of a tithe due to the king. It is believed to be have originated in the year 1500.

*Paying, therefore the several duties, after specifies, viz. for
the said lands and Barony of Carnwath, comprehending as
aforesaid, one pair of hose containing half an ell of English
cloth upon the ground of the said Barony, at the feast of St John
the Baptist called midsummer, to any person running fastest
from the east end of the town of Carnwath to the Cross called
Cawlo Cross in name of blenchferme only.*

Charter of Carnwath, 1500

Silver bell

In Paisley on St James Day in August a foot-race was held for a
four-ounce silver bell gifted in 1608 by the Earl of Abercorn.
The starting point of the race was St Conval's stone or 'chariot'.

*At the gray stone callet St Conval's stone, and fra that richt
oot to the lytle hoose at the calsend of Renfrew and fra that
on the King's way to the Walneuk of Paislaye.*

The Borderlands of Glasgow, T.C.F. Brotchie, 1923

Brewster wives race

In 1661 a foot-race was run by twelve brewster-wives [ale-
wives] 'all of them in a condition which makes violent exertion
unsuitable to the female frame' from the Figgat Burn to the
top of Arthur's Seat, Edinburgh, for a groaning cheese of one
hundred pounds in weight for the winner and a 'budgell [bottle]
of Dunkeld aquavitae and rumpkin of Brunswick Mum' as
second prize given by the Dutch midwife. The next day sixteen
fish-wives trotted from Musselburgh to the Canon Cross for
twelve pairs of harrigalls 'the entrails and offal of sheep'.

Hat and Ribbon Race

The winner of a foot race which was held, annually, originally for
herd laddies, at Inverkeithing, always received a hat and ribbons
which he gave to his sweetheart. This took place on the opening
day of the Lammas Fair, the first of August. It developed, in
recent years, into a ceremony with a civic procession. The Burgh
Officer led this, carrying the top hat, known as a lum or tile hat.
This was mounted, with the ribbons, onto a halberd and held
aloft as, accompanied by a brass band, it was paraded for all to
see. The race was through the streets for about a mile.

Biggar
At Biggar on the day of St Peter's Fair, held in July since the sixteenth century, a pair of gloves, given by Lord Fleming was awarded to the winner of a foot-race through the town.

Kilmarnock bonnets
In both Eaglesham and Kilmarnock awards of Kilmarnock bonnets awaited the winner of the foot-race. At Kilmarnock a pair of breeches, a purse of leather and the bonnet were attached to a halberd and paraded through the town while at Eaglesham it was the bonnet worn by the oldest feuar in the Riding of the Marches procession, which was presented to the winner.

Jedburgh
Athletes require to be early risers in Jedburgh as the town race takes place at 6.00 a.m. on the day of the Riding of the Marches. Jedburgh Border Games is the largest athletic meeting in Scotland with crowds of up to five thousand people attending.

Pollockshaws
The Maxwells of Pollok were granted a Charter for a Burgh of Barony to be called Pollockshaws, in 1814. Races were held in Pollok Estate on the days of the Shaw's Fair in July.

Kipper Fair
This was a fair held at Ayr, up until the 1830s, at the end of the salmon fishing season. Free smoked salmon was served in the public houses and foot-races were held between the 'cadgers', as the fish carriers were called.

Mauchline
At Mauchline fair foot races were held and Robert Burns mentions one of the main contenders, Racer Jess, the daughter of Poosie Nancy in his poem the 'Holy Fair' written in 1785.

Queensferry
At South Queensferry a pair of boots, given as a prize by the Town Council, were carried on a halberd and presented to the winner of the road race. This was originally held on the twenty-fifth of July, the day of the St James Fair, but was later transferred to the fourth of August during the Burryman's procession.

174

Horse races

Horse races were popular at festivals and fairs and gradually developed into an independent sport. David Home of Wedderburn collected eight of the swiftest horses from England and in 1574 he raced these at Haddington and won many prizes. Habbie Simson, the piper of Kilbarchan played regularly at horse races.

And at Horse Races many a day,
Before the black, the brown, the gray,
He gart his pipe, when he did play,
Baith skirl and skreed,
Now all such pastimes' s quite away,
Sen Habbie's dead.

The Life and Death of the Piper of Kilbarchan, Sir Robert Sempill ofBeltrees, from *Poems of the Sempills of Beltrees*, James Patterson, 1849

Leith

In March 1661 races took place at Leith on a regular basis. The races were held from the twentieth to the twenty-fourth of July.

Our accustomed recreations on the sands of Leith was much
hindered because of a furious storm of wind, accompanied
with a thick snow; yet we have had some noble gamesters that
were so constant in their sport as would not forbear a designed
horse-match. It was a providence the wind was from the sea;
otherwise they had run a hazard of either drowning or splitting
upon Inchkeith.

Domestic Annals of Scotland, Vol. 2, From the Revolution to the Rebellion 1745, Robert Chambers, 1874

One of the main prizes was a purse of a hundred guineas gifted by the king. The races opened with a procession and there was a fair with refreshments available held during the same period

Whan on Leith-Sands the racers rare,
Wi' jockey louns are met,
Their orro pennies there to ware,
And drown themselves in debt
Fu' deep that day . . .
The races o'er, they hale the dools,
Wi' drink o' a' kin-kind;

Great feck gae hirpling hame like fools
The cripple lead the blind.
May ne'er the canker o' the drink
E'er make our spirits thrawart,
Case we git wharewitha' to wink
Wi' een as blue's a blawart
Wi' straiks thir days!

Leith Races, Robert Fergusson, 1773

The races were moved from the Leith Sands in 1816 to the Links and became the Musselburgh Racecourse jointly managed by the Committee under the Earl of Rosebery and Musselburgh town council. In 1986 a winter jumps course was added to the flat racing course making it an all-year-round racecourse.

Cupar

Horse races were held annually, in April, at Cupar, Fife. They first began in 1621 when the Lairds of Philiphaugh, Stobbs and Powrie brought horses to race for a large silver cup, valued at £18 Scots. At one of these races held at Cupar in 1666, Lord Lithgow and Lord Carnegie took part in a duel. Swords were drawn and two horses were killed in a fight. Both gentlemen were arrested by the Earl of Rothes, the High Commissioner, and detained at the King's pleasure.

Duke of Hamilton

Horse-racing was a favourite pasttime, in the nineteenth century, of the Duke of Hamilton who gave it his patronage. He held annual races in the grounds of Hamilton Palace. Hamilton Racecourse is still one of the foremost courses in Scotland.

At that time the Duke and Mr Newbyth were leading men
on the turf; and in 1791 the famous match betwixt the two
individuals was run over the celebrated course at Hamilton.

Glasgow and Its Clubs, John Strang, 1856

Shaw's Fair

Pollockshaws, a village in its own right in the nineteenth century, now a part of Glasgow, held races in Pollok Estate during the Shaw's fair.

I thocht unto mysel' ae day I'd like tae see a race,
And for the best o' sport I'm telt, the Shaws is jist the place;
Sae up I gat up an' was'd mysel', put on my Sunday braws,
An' wi' a stick into my hand I started for the Shaws!
My mither telt me tae behave an' mind whit I'm aboot,
For there were queer folk in the Shaws, as I wud soon fin' oot.
Said she, 'Ye may be trod tae daith beneath the horses' paws,
An' mind, ye lad, the sayin's true – There's queer folk in the
     Shaws.'

The races pleased me unco weel – losh! they were grand to see,
The horses ran sae awfu' swift, I thocht they maist did flee.
When they cam' near the winnin' post – o, siccan loud hurrahs!
Ye wad hae thocht they'd a' gane daft – the queer folk in the
     Shaws.

Traditional

Marymas races

The oldest horse races were held at Marymas at Ayr. Except
for one or two modest plate events most of these races were
confined to cart horses, plough horses and other honest creatures
who have to fulfil some such conditions as 'must be the bonafide
property of Brothered Carters' and have regularly carted in
town or halfway within a radius of thirty miles.

Sunday Times, 15th August 1953

Other horse races were held at Kilmarnock on Irvine Moor at
Marymas and at Mauchline.

Betting

Placing a wager on the outcome of a horse race was seen as an
evil and there were many laws passed against it. The amount of
the stake in the nineteenth century was limited to 100 merks.
Up until after the Second World War off-course betting was
illegal and bookies' runners, who stood on corners and took
bets were regularly arrested and fined.

Riding the Marches

Through time horse races became attached to many of the
inspections of the boundaries. Most of them included tough

terrain and those who took part needed to be good horsemen and in some cases, women.

> *Amongst those riding the marches there sprang up, not unnaturally, a spirit of competition as to the mettle of their mounts, and the races which resulted were at first confined to animals which had gone round the boundaries.*
>
> Langholm, J. & R. Hyslop, 1912

Peebles

At Peebles during the Beltane festival ladies take to the saddle in the Ladies' Scamper and attempt to win the Royal Burgh of Peebles Callant's Club Trophy. Another ancient trophy in Peebles is the Beltane Bell, raced for during the Cornet's Canter and presented as the final act of the Riding of the Marches ceremonies.

Donkey races

At the Kipper Fair, at Ayr in August, the cadgers raced their donkeys and cart horses, up to two hundred of them, along the shore. They sat facing the tail of the donkey.

HIGHLAND GAMES

Highland Games were a throwback to the fourteenth and fifth-teenth centuries in the Highlands, when the young clansmen took part in refining their martial skills by practising swimming, wrestling, dancing and fencing. The games held at Strathfillan in 1826 among the oldest in Scotland held as an organized competition in the modern form which included playing the bagpipes and dancing as well as the athletic sports. The Northern Meeting at Inverness [1788] begs to claim that title.

> *The Northern Meeting, the oldest of the Highland gatherings, is generally held in the third week of September. The venue of the famous Highland gathering is the Northern Meeting Park, on the Western bank of the Ness and close to the Cathedral. Some of Scotland's most famous athletes, dancers and pipers, participate in the competition which is as keen as it is exhilarating.*
>
> Book of the Highlands, Official Guide to Inverness, 1933

Today many towns hold Highland Games which are now as likely to have professional competitors from the Lowlands as true physical specimens of Highland life.

Field events
Throwing the hammer
The blacksmith used a heavy sledgehammer in his work. The local youths who gathered at the smiddy borrowed this and challenged each other as to who could throw it the farthest. From this a competitive athletic event developed called throwing the hammer. The hammer used in the nineteenth century was a 'forehammer' which had a peculiarly shaped head. This was eventually changed into an iron ball of a standard weight of sixteen and twenty-two pounds which was attached to a wooden shaft. The thrower stands with his back to the stance and with his feet firmly placed on the ground. He swings the hammer around his head until he builds up a rhythmic speed when he lets go and it flies through the air.

Putting the stone
Originally young men lifted smooth stones from the river bed and threw them just for fun. Through time this was incorporated into the games and the stones had to be a standardized weight. The weights were sixteen or twenty-eight pounds. Known in athletics as putting the shot this has always been a popular event at Highland games. It is an event which requires strength and good balance. The thrower stands behind a wooden block onto which he must not put his foot and, swaying backwards and forwards, lets his stone go.

Tossing the caber
The art of tossing the caber was originally a practical one which was used when tree trunks had to be placed upright to form the supports of a house. Firstly the tree trunk had to be brought from the wood and the easiest way to move it over uneven ground was by constantly turning it over and over. The caber is a smooth tree trunk of about seventeen to twenty feet in length and weighs around one hundred and twenty to one hundred and thirty pounds. The object of the toss is to make the caber stand at an angle of ninety degrees to the ground. The caber is

lifted by the competitor and tossed so that it turns a full circle and must land upright with the thickest end downwards.

> *The games, which had been mounting in interest throughout the day, took on a new excitement as the contest to toss the giant Braemar Caber got under way. This gigantic pine trunk is just under twenty feet long and weighs over 130 pounds. Urged on by the roars of the crowd – and the obvious encouragement of not only the younger members of the Royal party! – the athletic giants Bill Anderson and Arthur Rowe successfully tossed the monster caber.*
>
> Programme of the Braemar Gathering, 1967

A prize of £10 was awarded to the winner.

Pole vaulting
This was another event which had a practical origin. When armies came up against moats or castle walls they had to find a way over them. Some intrepid soldiers would take a run at the obstacle carrying a wooden pole and propel themselves upwards and across by sticking the end of this into the ground. The athlete at the games emulated this feat and the winner not only jumped the highest but had to land upright on the turf.

Jumping
Competitions for the high jump, the long jump and hop, step and jump take place. These activities originated in the crossing of rugged terrain and the need to go over walls. Professional athletes travel the games circuit in the summer months to compete in these events all over Scotland.

Cumberland wrestling
The form of wrestling used at Highland games originated over the border in the Lake District of England. It has specific rules and is an art compared with all-in wrestling. One hand must be over the opponents shoulder and the other underneath the opponents oppposite arm with the hands clasped behind his back. If this grip is broken, a fall is declared in favour of the opponent. The idea is to force the opponent to touch the ground with a part of his body other than his feet. The best of three falls wins.

Tug of War

This is a team event which is always popular. Two teams of equal numbers take hold of a rope from the middle. Competitors are placed one behind the other, on each side of the centre mark, at a space of two feet. At a signal the team heaves, with the object of pulling their opponents over the mark onto their side of it. It is a feat of strength and rythmic movement which causes great excitement as the teams struggle to preserve their own position while at the same time ensuring that their opponents are pulled across to their side.

Track events

Foot-races, both short sprints on the flat and over hurdles as well as longer races, including steeplechases and obstacle races take place. These developed from the necessity for those Highlanders who served as messengers of their clan to be fleet of foot and hill races are a direct descendant of the lighting of the fiery cross on the hilltops by which means clansmen could be summoned in time of war.

Piping

At Highland games one of the best supported classes is that of playing the bagpipes. Bagpipe music was banned in Scotland in 1747 after the Jacobite Rebellions. This did not succeed in killing off the practice even though the sentence was six months in jail for a first offence and transportation abroad for seven years for any future transgression. When, in 1782, the ban was lifted, piping again became popular and young men who had learned to play – privately if not on official occcasions – during the ban, joined experienced practioners.

> *Music first on earth was found*
> *In Gaelic accent deep;*
> *When Jubal in his oxter sqeezed*
> *The blether o' a sheep.*
>
> Traditional

Pibroch

The pibroch, which is the *'ceol mor'* or great music, has a main theme called the *'urlar'*, with a series of variations and can be a lament for the dead or a salute to the living.

Medal for the best pibroch

The Highland Society of London awarded annually the prizes given by the London Society for the encouragement of bagpipe music at the Falkirk Tryst.

> *The competition for the annual prizes given by the Highland Society, for the encouragement of the ancient martial music of Scotland took place at Falkirk, on Wednesday, the fifteenth current, under the direction of a committee deputed by the Glasgow branch of the Society when after a trial of skill, which lasted from nine in the morning till five in the afternoon before select judges, and in the presence of numerous and respectable company assembled on this occasion the prizes were adjudged . . . The whole was concluded with a grand procession to the churchyard of Falkirk, where the victors at the three competitions, marched thrice round the tombs of the immortal heroes, Sir John Stuart, Sir John, the Graham and Sir Robert Munro playing the celebrated 'McCrimmons Lament' in concert on the prize pipes.*
>
> Glasgow and Its Clubs, John Strang, 1864

Ceol artrum

The *'ceol artrum'* is lighter music and consists of marches, strathspeys and reels. Solo pipers compete against each other, usually playing three pieces which they nominate beforehand.

Pipe-band contests

These are held throughout the country and bands come from abroad to take part. Some are incorporated into Highland games. Women pipers are now often included in the bands although traditionally it was a male preserve. As well as regiments other organizations have pipe bands. Many works had pipe bands, miners, the police, the youth organisations and towns and districts. They dress in full highland dress and the blaze of colour is impressive.

Cowal Gathering

At the annual Cowal Gathering held in Dunoon, in August, one of the highlights is the march of the pipe bands with over one thousand pipers playing on their way to and from the pier to the sports ground. An international field of pipers, pipe-bands and dancers enter the competitions.

Braemar Gathering

The March of the Massed Pipe Bands takes place at noon and again at three o'clock. This is a remnant of the once splendid March of the Clansmen. The Royal Highlanders from Balmoral carried Lochaber battle axes, the Duff Highlanders bore pikes over their shoulders and the Invercauld Highlanders carried swords. Each clan, headed by its pipers playing their distinctive tunes marched to the Gathering. It ceased in the reign of King George V with the disbanding of these regiments.

Highland dancing

Dancing the exacting steps is an art which has been handed down for generations. Many of the dances have origins from the twelfth century while others are the products of the eighteenth century. Traditionally Highland dancing was a male-only affair but for many years girls have taken part wearing the kilt. In 1952 an attempt was made to revive the original type of dress which was more acceptable to the traditionalists but both forms co-exist. There are still men-only and boys-only competitions.

The sword dance

This dance, the Ghillie Callum or sword dance, is attributed to King Malcolm Ceann Mor who is believed to have laid his sword on the ground across that of his dead enemy and proceeded to dance a dance of victory over them. The dancer must not touch the blades of the sword but carefully and speedily dance in between them.

The Reel of Tulloch

This is a sword dance performed by four men around one set of swords and has very fast steps. Legend attributed this dance to clansmen on Deeside stamping their feet and flailing their arms to keep warm when it was very cold. Both these sword dances were 'Righil a' Thulaichen' – Hullachan' [a Highland Reel] and they are believed to have a religious significance going back to Celtic times.

The 'Seann Truibhas'

The Gaelic word for old breeks or trousers was 'truibhas' or 'trews'. This dance originated after the Jacobite Rebellions when the ban on the wearing of the kilt was imposed. The dance begins with slow graceful strathspey steps and moves on to a faster step.

The Highland Fling

This dance is of fairly modern origin, being first danced in 1792 in honour of Jean, Duchess of Gordon and the raising of the Gordon Highlanders. It has a fast pace and intricate steps.

Young dancers

At Braemar there is a Challenge Shield presented by a New Zealander to the Best Boy Dancer under sixteen years of age and the Farquharson Sash and Kindrochit Brooch is won by the local girl dancer under twelve years of age with the most points.

Braemar Gathering

Although Strathfillan claims its gathering, in 1817, to be the first based on modern lines it was Queen Victoria's interest in the gathering at Braemar which ensured that it became the major one in Scotland. Since 1848 it has been attended by members of the Royal family and has been sneeringly accused of Balmorality by those who feel that it is a showpiece for the romanticized view of Scotland depicted by Sir Walter Scott.

The Braemar Wrights' Society which held an annual walk in 1816 with its members parading in long white linen aprons also held games and races after the event. The first of these was held in 1817 and is claimed as the original Braemar Highland Gathering. The Braemar Wrights Society developed into a Friendly Society which dissolved in 1826 but rose again as the Braemar Highland Society. This Society held its first gathering in August 1832 with a total prize-list of £5. In August 1848, Queen Victoria came to Balmoral and the date of the gathering at Invercauld House was altered to the middle of September when the Queen and Prince Albert could attend. Ever since, the monarch has been consulted as to the exact date of the gathering.

The gathering used to move around – one year held at Invercauld House, another at Braemar Castle, Mar Lodge or

Cluny Park. In 1886 Queen Victoria honoured the Society with her patronage and Royal was added to its title. The following year she invited the members of the Braemar Royal Highland Society to lunch and dinner and offered Balmoral as a venue for the gathering. It was held at Balmoral on a few occasions up until 1906 when it moved to its permanent home on the Moor of Wailing, gifted by the Duke of Fife and named 'The Princess Royal Park', after the Duchess of Fife, his wife. On their deaths it became The 'Princess Royal and Duke of Fife Memorial Park'. In 1900 at the request of Queen Victoria there was no gathering as a sign of respect for those servicemen killed during the Boer War.

Some of the competitions are limited to local competitors who must have been residents for at least six months in the Parishes of Glenmuick, Tullich and Glengairn, Crathie and Braemar or Glenshie or who qualify by birth.

The Alternative Scottish Games

These games began at Parton, in Galloway, in 1981, as a fun evening to raise money for charity. They have gone from strength to strength and in 1995 raised over £3000 for good causes. Instead of the traditional events the World Championship is awarded for the gird an' cleek race. This is an iron hoop with an attached handle through which the hoop can turn. The Balmaclellan Skittles are played, these are replicas of a set found perfectly preserved in a peat bog and are now in Dumfries Museum. Tossing the herd's bunnet, tossing the sheaf and other feats are rewarded with prizes of a dumpling , a mutton pie, a haggis or a joint of lamb complete with a bag of potatoes and a bag of peas. A leg of mutton is the prize for climbing the greasy pole and competitors may breed their own snails for the snail races.

A wide variety of events take place in towns and villages throughout Scotland during the year – games and gatherings, athletic meetings, miners' galas, civic weeks, the Gaelic Mod, jazz and other music and performing arts festivals; there are even flounder tramping and many other intriguing entertainments. Scottish Tourist Board Information Centres will have all the details.

Glossary

A

a'	all
a' body	everybody
aboon	above
accompts	accounts
actit	acted
aiblins	maybe, perhaps
ain	one, one's own
ane an' a'	everybody
anither	another
aquavitae	spirits, especially whisky
arles	money given to ensure service
aroon	around
arrest	seize
aucht	eigth
auld	old
auld claes and porridge	reality
aulden	olden
avocation	vow
awa'	away
awmous	alms
axle-tree	wooden axle

B

babblement	foolish nonsense
bairnies	children
baith	both
baith for bed an' for back	for home and clothing
baldric	holder for a sword
bannock	oatcake
bauld	bold
bawbee	coin
baxters	bakers
beir	beer
besoms	brooms
big	grown-up
birkie's	young upstarts
birkin bush	birch
birks	birch trees
bivouac	shelter
black-guardism	rascally behaviour,
bladder	sheep's stomach
blashy	gusty
blaw	blow

blawart	harebell/ bluebell
blenchferme	nominal rent
blether	chatter/gossip
bluid	blood
blythness	gladness
bogles	ghosts
boll	measure
bonafide	genuine
bothy	rough shelter
bourocks	house
bra'	fine
braw	best clothes
brecons	bracken
bricht	bright
briest	breast
broad-tail'd coat	long coat with tails
brochans	thin porridge and honey
brose caups	wooden cup for brose
browster wives	brewers of ale
bruckelie	weak/crumbly
Brunswick Mum	a type of ale
busk	make ready
butts	place for shooting practice

C

ca's	calls
cadger/caird/ carteris	carter
cald	cold

callant's	young men
caller	fresh
canny	careful
carabines	type of gun
carvie kebbuck,	type of cheese
caudles	egg mixture
chanticleers	cockerels
chawmir	room
chiel	person
chop	shop
claes	clothes
clout	cloth
cobbles	individual stones
cogs	wooden bowls
coining	forging money
cokalorum	silly
commonities	common ground
convoyed	walked beside
coonted	counted
crack	gossip/talk
crammed	crowded
crawl	throat/crow
cruzie	oil lamp
cuddies	horses
curds and quhey	curds and whey
curiously	well expressed

D

dadjell	to saunter
danner	to dawdle
darkenin'	twilight/dusk
dasses	steps
dee	die
deil	devil
diet hour	mealtime

dinlin	tingling sensation
dinna	do not
divertisement	entertainment
divination	future foretold
don	put on
drap	drop
drenched	soaked with water/rain
dusht	strike

E

een	eyes
efter	after
eidentl	diligently
eke	incite
ell	measure
entrance	to charm
equipage	full-dress

F

faes	foes
fairn-year	last year
faither	father
fal-de-rals	fripperies
fan	find
farmtoun	area around a farm
featly	neatly
feck	amount, bulk
ferlies	wonders
fiddlesticks	bow for playing violin
fiere	friend
firlot	measure
flaggon	metal drinking vessel
fleech	coax, flatter

fleshers	butchers
florrie	vain
fock	folk
fou	full
fou as a witch	drunk
fra	from
furnish	supply
fusees	type of gun
fustian	type of cloth
fyl'd	dirtied, soiled
fyreing of pieces	shooting

G

gane	gone
gang	go to
garred	made
gaun	going
gauntlets	long-cuffed gloves
gear	stuff
geir	goods
gew-gaws	trifles
gi'en	given
gibbet	gallows
gies	gives
gif	if, whether
gigs	small carriages
gin	if
glawr	mud
glumfie	moody, grumpy
glut	gulp, swallow
goldspinks	type of bird
goon	dress
gorget	collar
gowd	gold
gowk	cuckoo, a daftie
graithed	made ready

grieve	farm supervisor
gruel	thin porridge
guard	nightwatchman
gude	good
gudeman	husband
gudewife	wife
guid	good
guising	going out in disguise
gusty	windy

H

hads	holds
hail	whole
halberd	staff
halding	holding
hale	whole
hale the dools	unhappy
happer	hopper
hap-warms	plaid or warm clothes
hauberk	staff
haun	hand
hawked	sold
heckle	ask questions
heritor	landowner
herd/ herdsman	looks after animals
hicht	height
hiest pain	most painful
hindmost	last
hirpling	limping
hirstle	wheeze
hitch	tie-up
hiv	have
holden	held

horse-couper	horse-dealer
hurdie-gurdies	barrel organs

I

ilka	every
Italian tricks	type of music

J

jacks	small stones/ pebbles
Jeannies	country lassies
Jezebels	brazen women
Jocks and Jennies	farm/country servants

K

kail	colewart
kent	knew
kens	knows
kickshaws	novelties
kin-kind	relatives
kintra	country
kits	wooden drinking cups
kye	cattle

L

laird o' the soil	landowner
land-loupers	vagabonds
lang's	long as
lawn	grassland
leading grain	harvested grain
leavin'	leaving
leddies	ladies
lee	lie

Lentron	at Lent
lisk	flank
Lockerby	Lockerbie
loose boys	dishonest rascals
losh	exclamation
louns	young men
lyin' in the clay	dead
lyke-wake	lying with the corpse
lytle	little

M

maid	made
malefactor	evil-doer
Maraschino di Zara	Italian wine
marrow	sweetheart
maun	must
meen	moon
micht	might
moleskins	trousers made of that material
mony	many
morn	morning/the next day
mou	mouth
muckle	big, large

N

naething	nothing
ne'er	never
neast	next, nearest
neebor	neighbour
nickering	neighing
nippin	tingling
noggin	small wooden bowl

O

'oo	wool
oot	out
or	gold
ordinance	communion of the Church of Scotland
orro	extra
ouzily	unkempt, slovenly
oxter	armpit

P

partriks	partridges
paynteris	painters
perambulat	strolled
Pess	Easter
plai	sport
platter	wooden plate
pleys	dramatic play
ploo	plough
pokey hat	ice-cream cone
poniard	sword
pouches	pockets
praisit	praised
pu	pull
puddins	white (oatmeal,) black, or haggis
pun	pound

Q

quarter day	term or rent days
quern	hollow stone for grinding corn
quha	what

R

rabblement	confused chatter
raise	rise
ravelling	tangling
ravishing	starving
reaming	overflowing
riband	ribbon
rid	red
riddles	puzzles
rin	run
rin wrang	go the wrong way
roset	rosin, for waxing violin bows
rumpkin	measure

S

Sabbath rest	Sunday break
sair'd	ached
saps	bread and milk
sauty	salty
scantlin	scarce
scramble	disorderly
seasons of sacrament	Holy Communion
sely	happy
sen	since
set on	employed
shanks	legs
shielings	summer pastures
shilling bit	coin
shoon	shoes
sic	such
siccan	such an/such as
sicht	sight
sick	such
siller	silver

sixpence	coin
skaith	damage/injury
skits	practical jokes
skruchs	screeches
sma'	small
sma' beer	light beer
Sol	sun
sonsy	lucky/saucy
soum	swim
soume	some
soup	sup
speen	spoon
speir	ask
spulying	plundering
squabblement	disturbing the peace
stamacks	stomachs
stammer	stagger/stumble
starnies	stars
staun	staun
steerin'	stirring
steeve	stiff/stubborn
stirred a fit	rose
stitch	pain in the side
stiveron	fat food/a haggis
stook	hay piled up in a cone
store	goods
stoup	jug with a handle
stow'd	put away/ furnished
straiks	strokes
straths	valleys
swatch	sample
sweeled	whirled around
sweetmeats	sweeties and cakes

synd	rinsed
syne	long ago/since

T

tawties	potatoes
tee	to
Terpsichore	goddess of dance
thesaurer	treasurer
thochts	thoughts
thrawart	twisted
tillage	cultivation
tilting	running at
tinkers	gypsy/metal worker
tip	tap
tither	other
toddy	drink/whisky, sugar and hot water
tron	weighbridge
trow	trust
trumps	cheats
Tulloch Gorum	pipe tune
tuppence, twapenny	two pennies

U

umberell	umbrella
unco	great/very

W

wae	woe
wallets	pedlars
wames	stomachs
ware	worn
was'd	washed
wee sma' hours	early hours of the morning
weel	well
weet	wet
weid	garment
weir-men	soldiers
wharewitha'	wherewithal
whaur	where
whilk	which
whiteairn	hot iron
whomeld owre	tumbled
widdershins	anti-clockwise
widna	would not
willie waught	serious drinking
wud	would

Y

yince	once
yont	yonder/beyond

Festivals and Celebrations

January 1st	New Year's Day
January 1st	Ba' Game, Kirkwall
January 1st	Boys' Walk, Dufftown
January 1st	Yetlins, East Weems
January 2nd	Handsell Monday
January 6th	Uphallie Day
January 11th	Burning the Clavie
January 12th	Old New Year's Day
January 25th	Burns' Night
January – last Tuesday	Up Helly-aa, Lerwick
February 1st	St Bride's Day
February 2nd	Candlemas
February 2nd	Candlemas Ba', Jedburgh
Thursday before Lent	Fastern's E'en
Thursday before Lent	Fastern's E'en Ba', Jedburgh
Thursday before Lent	Beef Brose and Bannock Night
Thursday before Lent	Rappy Night
February 14th	St Valentine's Day
March 1st	Whuppity Scourie
March 30th	Taillie Day
Moveable feasts	Easter/ Pasch
	Good Friday
	Horse and Plough, Orkney
	Gyro Night, Orkney

April 1st	Huntigowk
April	Links Market, Kirkcaldy
April	Kate Kennedy, St Andrews
May 1st, 3rd, 8th	Beltane
May 1st	May Day
May 1st	Robin Hood Games
May 3rd	Rood Day in barlan
May	Lanimer Week, Lanark
May 24th	Victoria Day
May 24th	Empire Day
May 29th	King's Birthday
June	Carter and Whipman Plays
June – various dates	Riding the Marches
June	Newland Day, Bathgate
June 21st	Midsummer's Eve
June	Bannockburn Rally, Bannockburn
June 24th	St John's Eve
June 25th	Whitsun
June	Guid Nychburris, Dumfries
June 29th	Petermas
July 15th	Martin Bullion's Day
July	Douglas Day, Castle Douglas
July	Cleikum Ceremony, St Ronan's
June	Herring Queen, Wick
August 1st	Lammas
August First Saturday	Fish Festival, Pittenweem
August First Sunday	Scottish Alternative Games, Parton
August	Flodden Ride, Coldstream
August	Flounder Tramping, Palnackie
August Second Week	Burryman Procession
August 15th	Marymas
August 15th	Arbroath Pageant
August 23rd	Wallace Day, Elderslie
August	Lilias' Day, Kilbarchan
September – various dates	Fishermen's Walks
September 25th	Rood Day in hairst
September 27th	Feast of St Barr

September 28th	Michaelmas Eve
September 29th	St Michael's Day
October 18th	St Luke's Eve
October 18th	Sour Cakes Day
October 30th	Batter-Door-Night
October 31st	Hallowe'en
November 1st	All Saints Day
November 5th	Bonfire Night
November 5th	Popnight, Orkney
November 11th	Martinmas
November 11th [nearest Sunday]	Armistice Day
November 30th	St Andrew's Day
December 6th	St Nicholas Eve
December 21st	St Thomas Day
December 21st	Barring-out Day
December 24th	Christmas Eve
December 25th	Christmas Day
December 26th	Sweetie Scone Day
December 26th	Innocents' Day
December 27th	Masons' Walk, Melrose
December 29th-31st	Torchlight Procession & Hogmany Party, Edinburgh
December 31st	Hogmanay
December 31st	Cake Night
December 31st	Fireballs, Stonehaven
December 31st	Flambeaux, Comrie

Saint's Name	Fair Name (if different)	Place	Month
Alexander		Keith	May
Adamnan		Dull	September
Angus		Kingshouse	August
Barr		Dornoch	September
Barr		Eddleston	September
Berchan	St Barchan's	Kilbarchan	August
Berchan	St Barquhan's	Tain	August
Boisil	St Boswell's	St Boswell's	February
Boniface		Fortrose	July
Brendan	St Birnie's	Kilbirnie	May
Brendan		Inveraray	May
Brendan		Barra	May
Brioc	St Brock's	Rothesay	April
Brioc	Brux Day	Millport	April
Callen		Rogart	November
Causnan	St Cousland's	Dunnichen	March
Columba		Aberdour	June
Columba		Dunkeld	June
Columba		Drymen	June
Columba	St Colm's	Largs	June
Columba		Fort-Augustus	June
Comgall		Durris	May
Comgan	Cowan	Turriff	October
Conan		Glenorchy	January
Cuthbert		Ruthwell	March
Cuthbert		Kirkcudbright	March
Cuthbert		Ordiquhill	March
Devenick	Dennick's	Milton of Glenesk	November
Donnan	Donan	Auchterlees	April
Donnan	Donan	Kildonan	April
Drostan		Rothiemay	July
Drostan		Aberlour	July
Drostan		Old Deer	July
Duthac	St Duthac in Lent	Tain	March

Saint's Name	Fair Name (if different)	Place	Month
Duthac		Tain	December
Ethernan	Tuetherean's	Forfar	December
Ethernan	Tuetherean's	Madderty	December
Eunan		Blair Atholl	September
Fergus	Fergusmas	Glamis	November
Fergus	Fergusmas	Wick	November
Fillan		Houston	February
Fillan		Struan	February
Finan	St Finzean's	Perth	March
Finan		Glenfinnan	March
Finian	Finzean	Migvie	March
Fumac		Botriphnie	May
Fumac		Dinet	May
Fyndoca		Findogask	October
Gilbert		Dornoch	April
Giles		Moffat	September
Giles		Elgin	September
Inan	Tenant's	Inchinnan	August
Machan		Clachan of Campsie	October
Machan		Kilmahog	October
Magnus	Magnusmas	Watten-Wester	April
Malloch	Mallock's	Clatt	June
Maree/ Maelrubha/ Murie/		Forres	April
Maree/as above	Summer Eve's	Keith	September
Maree/as above	August Market	Dingwall	August
Maree/as above	Lairg	April	
Maree/as above	Pitlessie	April	
Margaret	Margaretmas	Wick	November
Margaret	Margaretmas	Closeburn	November
Margaret	Margaretmas	Thornhill (Balquapple)	November
Marnoch	Marnock	Paisley	March

Saint's Name	Fair Name (if different)	Place	Month
Marnoch	Marnock	Aberchirder	March
Marthom		Ordiquhill	September
Methven	Methvenmas	Fowlis-Wester	September
Mirrin		Paisley	September
Mittan		Kilmaddock	February
Moluag	Luoch	Tarland	July
Moluag	St Malogue's	Alyth	July
Monoch	Sam Meneuke's (St Monk)	Stevenson	October
Mund		Kilmun	April
Mungo		Alloa	January
Nathalan		Old Meldrum	January
Nathalan		Cowie	January
Ninian		Whithorn	September
Ninian		Arbroath	September
Olaf	St Olla	Kirkwall	April
Olaf	St Ole	Cruden Bay	April
Palladius	Paldy	Fordoun	July
Patrick	Patrickmas	Dumbarton	March
Rule	Trewell	Kennethmont	October
Serf		Culross	July
Serf		Abercorn	July
Serf		Aberlednock	July
Talarican		Fordyce	October
Ternan		Banchory	June
Triduana	Trodlin's	Forfar	October
Virgin Mary	Marymas	Inverness	August
Virgin Mary	Marymas	Irvine	August

Short Bibliography

Barrett, Dom Michael *A Calendar of Scottish Saints*, 2nd edition, 1919.

Chambers, Robert *Domestic Annals of Scotland*, Vols 1–3, *From the Revolution to the Rebellion 1745*, W. & R. Chambers, 1874.

Ford, Robert, ed., *Vagabond Songs and Ballads*, Gardner, 1904.

Graham, H. G., *The Social Life of Scotland in the Eighteenth Century*, A. & C. Black, 1899.

Groome, F. H., ed., *Ordnance Gazetteer of Scotland: A Survey of Scottish Topography, Statistical, Biographical, and Historical*, Vols 1–6, Thomas C. Jack, 1882

Hole, Christina *Dictionary of British Folk Customs*, Hutchinson, 1976.

Lamont-Brown, Raymond, *Scottish Festivals and Traditions*, Chambers, 1992.

McNeill, F. M., *The Silver Bough*, Vols 1–4, Stuart Titles, 1957/68.

Napier, James, *Folklore and Superstitious Beliefs in the West of Scotland within this Century*, Gardner, 1879.

Sinclair, Sir John, ed., *First Statistical Account of Scotland*, 1796.

Sinclair, Sir John, ed., *Second Statistical Account of Scotland*, 1856.

Index